POPUL

Waterton Lakes National Park

ANDREW NUGARA

RMB

For information on purchasing bulk quantities of this book, or to obtain media excerpts or invite the author t
speak at an event, please visit rmbooks.com and select the "Contact" tab.

RMB | Rocky Mountain Books Ltd.
rmbooks.com
@rmbooks
facebook.com/rmbooks

Cataloguing data available from Library and Archives Canada
ISBN 9781771602693 (softcover)
ISBN 9781771602709 (electronic)

All photographs are by Andrew Nugara unless otherwise noted.

Printed and bound in China

We would like to also take this opportunity to acknowledge the traditional territories upon which we live and work. I
Calgary, Alberta, we acknowledge the Niitsitapi (Blackfoot) and the people of the Treaty 7 region in Southern Alberta
which includes the Siksika, the Piikuni, the Kainai, the Tsuut'ina and the Stoney Nakoda First Nations, includin
Chiniki, Bearpaw, and Wesley First Nations. The City of Calgary is also home to Métis Nation of Alberta, Region I
In Victoria, British Columbia, we acknowledge the traditional territories of the Lkwungen (Esquimalt, and Song
hees), Malahat, Pacheedaht, Scia'new, T'Sou-ke and W̱SÁNEĆ (Pauquachin, Tsartlip, Tsawout, Tseycum) peoples

We acknowledge the financial support of the Government of Canada through the Canada Book Fund and the Car
ada Council for the Arts, and of the province of British Columbia through the British Columbia Arts Council an
the Book Publishing Tax Credit.

Disclaimer

The actions described in this book may be considered inherently dangerous activities. Individuals undertake thes
activities at their own risk. The information put forth in this guide has been collected from a variety of sources an
is not guaranteed to be completely accurate or reliable. Many conditions and some information may change owin
to weather and numerous other factors beyond the control of the authors and publishers. Individuals or group
must determine the risks, use their own judgment, and take full responsibility for their actions. Do not depend o
any information found in this book for your own personal safety. Your safety depends on your own good judgmen
based on your skills, education, and experience.

It is up to the users of this guidebook to acquire the necessary skills for safe experiences and to exercise caution i
potentially hazardous areas. The authors and publishers of this guide accept no responsibility for your actions o
the results that occur from another's actions, choices, or judgments. If you have any doubt as to your safety or you
ability to attempt anything described in this guidebook, do not attempt it.

Contents

Area Map   4

Introduction   5

Using this book   8

Red Rock Parkway   10

  1 Bellevue Prairie Trail South   12
  2 Crandell Lake   14
  3 Lost Horse Creek   17
  4 Red Rock Canyon   20
  5 Goat Lake   24
  6 Sage Pass   32
  7 Blakiston Falls   39
  8 Blakiston Valley   43

Akamina Parkway   52

  9 Crandell Lake   54
 10 Lineham Falls   57
 11 Ruby Ridge   60
 12 Rowe Lakes   64
 13 Lineham Ridge   70
 14 Forum Lake   74
 15 Wall Lake   81
 16 Cameron Lakeshore   84
 17 Akamina Lake   86
 18 Summit Lake   88
 19 Carthew Summit   90
 20 Carthew–Alderson Lakes   95

Waterton Townsite   98

 21 Bear's Hump   100
 22 Linnet Lake and trails   103
 23 Crypt Lake   108
 24 Waterton Lakeshore   111
 25 Bertha Lake   113
 26 Bertha Bay   118
 27 Alderson Lake   122

Additional Routes   126

 28 Horseshoe Basin Loop Trail   128
 29 Bellevue Hill   136
 30 Bellevue Prairie Trail North   141
 31 Kootenai Brown Trail   143
 32 Vimy Peak   146
 33 Wishbone   152
 34 Sofa Mountain trail   156

Contact Information   160

Acknowledgements   160

Area Map

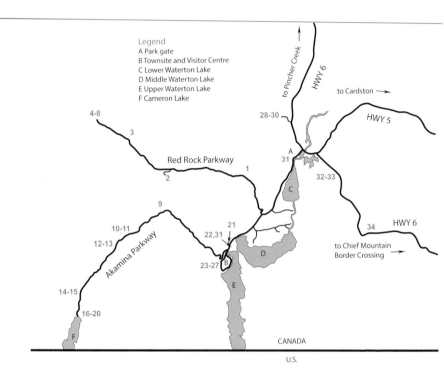

Legend
A Park gate
B Townsite and Visitor Centre
C Lower Waterton Lake
D Middle Waterton Lake
E Upper Waterton Lake
F Cameron Lake

to Pincher Creek
HWY 6
to Cardston →
HWY 5
28-30
4-8
3
Red Rock Parkway
A
31
1
2
32-33
C
9
21
10-11
22,31
12-13
Akamina Parkway
D
HWY 6
34
23-27 B
to Chief Mountain
Border Crossing →
E
14-15
16-20
F
CANADA
U.S.

Introduction

About Waterton Lakes National Park

Waterton is one of Alberta's hidden gems. Tucked in the far southwest corner of the province, within striking distance of both British Columbia and Montana, the park offers consistently spectacular scenery: mountain, lake and prairie. An excellent and extensive trail system allows hikers to explore much of this incredible environment with relative ease.

The town of Waterton sits near the shores of the deepest lake in the Canadian Rockies, the massive Upper Waterton Lake, at a maximum depth of 150 m. Smaller but equally scenic lakes abound throughout the park, most of them accessible by trail.

Another of the many highlights of Waterton is the rock. Waterton and its southerly neighbour, Glacier National Park in Montana, contain some of the most colourful and unique strata in the Rockies. Strikingly beautiful examples of red and green argillite (a rock formed from hardened mud) are prevalent throughout the park, as well as equally colourful formations of shale, dolostone and limestone.

Enjoy the wonders of this amazing and visually stunning national park!

Welcome to the new Waterton

In September 2017 a naturally occurring forest fire swept through Waterton Park – the Kenow wildfire. The blaze destroyed huge swaths of old forest and much of the park's infrastructure outside the townsite. However, nature and man have stepped up to the plate (nature especially) and rejuvenated the park in astonishing ways. In general, the terrain is now more open, revealing stunning vistas not previously seen. Lush green vegetation is thriving everywhere, beautiful wild flowers are even more prevalent in early July, and regrowth of the forest is well under way.

In addition, Parks Canada and the good folks of Waterton have repaved the major roads, parking areas have been expanded, and washroom facilities have increased in number and improved in quality. The new visitor centre, right in the townsite, is spectacular, and for the kids, stopping to play in the new waterpark is a "must-do"!

Note that campgrounds that are presently closed (Crandell Mountain, Crandell Lake, Goat Lake and Belly River) may re-open in the future.

Of course, as the natural restoration of the park continues, new obstacles such as fallen dead trees will invariably present different challenges to hiking in the park.

At present, however, if you thought the pre-fire Waterton was beautiful, wait until you see the new Waterton!

Getting there

See the area map on page 44. From the north and/or west, Waterton is accessed from Highway 6, via Pincher Creek. From the south and/or east, Waterton is accessed from Highway 5. The park is 30 minutes from Pincher Creek, 1.5 hours from Lethbridge and 3 hours from Calgary. Driving is the best way to get there. Note that Waterton is a national park and therefore you'll need a park pass to enter. A pass can be purchased at the park entrance.

Seasonal road closures

Red Rock Parkway is closed to motor vehicles from November 1 to the first weekend of May, subject to weather. Walking, biking or skiing the road is permitted. The last 2.5 km of Akamina Parkway is also closed from November 1 to the first weekend of May, subject to weather. When this stretch of road is closed, Akamina Pass and Cameron Lake can be accessed on foot, skis or snowshoes.

Facilities

During the summer months, Waterton offers a wide variety of hotels and motels to stay at, as well as a large campground. There are many restaurants, from casual to fine dining. The visitor centre is usually open from the second week of May to the second week of October. As of 2021, services during the winter months were very limited in Waterton. This may change in the future as more people begin to experience the sublime beauty of the park during the snowy months.

Weather

In general the summer months in Waterton are beautifully sunny and very warm (up to the mid-30s). However, the park is subject to very high winds. Check the forecast, with special attention to wind speeds, before coming down to the park.

Autumn can be exceptionally pleasant, with more moderate temperatures and extended periods of stable weather. The larches change colour in the last part of September and first part of October, making it an ideal time to visit the park.

Hiking opportunities are limited during the winter months, as the park usually gets a significant amount of snow. Ski touring and snowshoeing are great ways to explore Waterton from December to May.

Drinking water

To be safe, it is best to bring your own water, or that from hotels, campgrounds etc. Natural sources may be contaminated with *Giardia lamblia*, a parasite that can cause severe gastrointestinal problems. At higher elevations it is generally safer to drink from streams without treating the water. Filtering the water is also an option.

Wildlife concerns

Animals are abundant in Waterton. Deer routinely roam the streets and graze on the lawns within the townsite. Stay away from them and DO NOT feed any form of wildlife. Bear sightings are also quite common, especially while driving either of the parkways. Please obey the speed limits and keep an eye out for wildlife on the road. When hiking, make lots of noise to warn bears and other animals of your presence. Moose and elk can be aggressive in the fall, during mating season – steer well clear if you encounter them.

Unfortunately, another life form prevalent in Waterton is ticks. From March to the end of June these insects ravenously feed on any mammal they can sink their mouthparts into, humans included. Check yourself carefully after any early season hike.

Safety tips

- If you will be hiking alone, let someone know where you are going. Make lots of noise while you are hiking. Most bear attacks involve solo hikers travelling quietly
- Don't be lulled into a false sense of security because you are in a larger group. You still must make noise to warn bears and other wildlife of your presence.
- Carry bear spray and know how to use it.
- Consider using a personal locator device such as SPOT, in case of an emergency.
- Stay on designated trails unless you are experienced and/or familiar with the challenges of off-trail hiking/scrambling.
- Check the weather forecast in advance. Also, check the official Waterton Lakes National Park website www.pc.gc.ca/en/pn-np/ab/waterton and the visitor centre, 403-859-5133, waterton.info@pc.gc.ca, for trail conditions and for trail and area closures.
- Afternoon thunderstorms are common in the summer. Start early to avoid them

Campgrounds

There are two frontcountry campground inside the park (Waterton Townsite and Crandell Mountain) and two outside the park (Crooked Creek and Belly River).

- Waterton Townsite. Call 1-877-737-3783 or reserve online.

- Crandell Mountain (closed as of 2021 but may reopen in the future). No reservations; first come, first served. Fills up quickly during the summer months.
- Crooked Creek. Call 403-653-1100 or reserve online.
- Belly River (closed as of 2021 but may reopen in the future). Call 403-859-2224 or reserve online.

The park has nine backcountry campgrounds, two of which (Crandell Lake and Goat Lake) remain closed as of 2021. The others are Boundary Bay, Bertha Bay, Bertha Lake, Alderson Lake, Lone Lake, Twin Lakes and Snowshoe. Reserve online or call the visitor centre at 403-859-5133.

Ascents from various campgrounds

Although all the summits in this book can be completed as day trips, staying at one of the backcountry campgrounds is a good option for some of the longer ascents.

- **Lone Lake:** Lone Mountain, Kishinena Peak (from the south), Mount Bauerman.
- **Snowshoe and Twin Lakes:** Kishinena Peak (from the north), "Sage Pass Peak" and "Sage Senior," Mount Bauerman.
- **Goat Lake:** Avion Ridge, Newman Peak and "Newman Senior".
- **Alderson Lake:** Mounts Alderson and Carthew.

Using this book

How the trails were chosen

Given the small size of the park (505 square kilometres, in comparison to Banff National Park's 6641 square kilometres), Waterton has a relatively small number of hiking trails. However, all those trails have great scenery en route and/or great views at the end, and thus the 34 routes in this book represent almost all the hikes in Waterton. In addition, numerous trips to the summits of mountains are described for the advanced hiker/scrambler. Many of these trips involve trail-less travel up steep terrain and route-finding but are incredibly rewarding.

Trails

Parks Canada has done an outstanding job of creating an extensive system of trails throughout the park. Most of these trails are well marked, well signed and well maintained. Therefore, many of the route descriptions are brief, requiring very little detail. Even the routes without any signage are generally easy to follow.

Options

Text in other colours indicates an option to extend the trip and/or make a side trip: "Going farther…"

Distances

Distances represent the round-trip distance for each route, unless specified otherwise.

Height gain

Height gains represent the total elevation gain for each round trip, including any significant ups and downs along the way.

High point

Included only for those trips that require a moderate to significant height gain and/or reach a summit.

Rating

The ratings used in this book are Very easy, Easy, Moderate, Strenuous and Very strenuous. Qualifiers have been included with trips rated Strenuous and Very strenuous. That is, strenuous based on length or on steepness or on both length and steepness.

Season

This recommends which time of the year to do the trip. Note that late spring and/or early autumn snow can dramatically affect the length of the hiking season from year to year.

Difficulty

Describes conditions underfoot and the steepness of the grades. It is assumed that the trips are undertaken with good hiking conditions, but adverse weather or snow may elevate the rating. Scrambling sections in this book are generally defined as steep hiking, often without a trail, and/or ascending small rock steps where you may need to use your hands.

Sketch maps

Red lines indicate main trails. Dashed red lines indicate optional routes and/or Going Farther routes.

Will I need any other maps?

For all hikes in Waterton, it is highly recommended that you bring with you Gem-Trek's *Waterton Lakes National Park* topographical map. This waterproof map is very detailed and shows all the official and many unofficial trails in the park. The back of the map contains several trail descriptions, as well as other information about the park.

For NTS maps (National Topographic System), 82 H/04 Waterton Lakes and 82 G/01 Sage Creek will be useful.

If you are using technology, getting the Topo Maps Canada app on your iPhone is ideal. The app uses a satellite signal, not a cellphone signal, to pinpoint your exact location and then shows that location on a topographical map. Thus you can be far out of cellphone signal range but still determine your location. The maps in the app also show many of the trails in Waterton. (You may be able to find something similar for Android.)

What to wear

Hiking boots, as opposed to runners, are highly recommended for all the trails. If you are going off-trail for some of the more scrambly terrain, then a good pair of sturdy hiking boots is essential. Bring a rain jacket and warm clothes, as the weather can change dramatically and very quickly. For those hot summer days, bring sunscreen, a hat and bug-repellent.

Doing more

For more hiking opportunities similar to those in Waterton, grab your passport and head south across the border into the jewel of Montana, Glacier National Park. The system of trails in this park is staggering and hiking them will keep you occupied and mesmerized for years. Within Canada, Crowsnest Pass, Kananaskis Country, Banff, Lake Louise, Yoho, Jasper and many other regions offer the same quality of world-class hiking that is commonplace in Waterton. Check out other books in RMB's Popular Day Hikes series, specifically *Popular Day Hikes: The Castle and Crowsnest*, by Andrew Nugara; *Popular Day Hikes: Kananaskis Country*, by Gillean Daffern; and *Popular Day Hikes: Canadian Rockies*, by Tony Daffern. The *Canadian Rockies Trail Guide*, by Brian Patton and Bart Robinson (Summerthought, 2017), is another excellent hiking resource.

The logical extension of hiking is scrambling – getting to the top of a mountain without technical means (i.e., ropes and climbing equipment). Surprisingly, every single one of the 30 or so official mountains (depending on the definition of "official" you choose to adopt), has a scramble route to the top. Acquire copies of Alan Kane's *Scrambles in the Canadian Rockies, 3rd Edition* and Andrew Nugara's *More Scrambles in the Canadian Rockies, 3rd Edition* for detailed information and route descriptions.

RED ROCK PARKWAY

Red Rock Parkway is the most scenic drive in Waterton and provides access to eight of the trails in this book, as well as seven summits. The Parkway turn-off is located 4.4 km from the park gate. Again, a reminder that this road is inaccessible to motor vehicles from November to the first weekend of May. Walking, biking, skiing or snowshoeing the road are permitted, however.

The Nugara clan enjoying the superb scenery in Lost Horse Creek.

1 Bellevue Prairie Trail South

Where the prairies meet the mountains. A pleasant hike alongside the fascinating east face of Bellevue Hill. Great during sunrise.

DISTANCE 7 KM RETURN

HEIGHT GAIN MINIMAL

VERY EASY

FIRST WEEKEND OF MAY TO NOVEMBER

START: Drive 3 km along Red Rock Parkway and park at the signed Bellevue trailhead on the right-hand side on the road.

DIFFICULTY: An unmaintained but easy to follow trail for the first few kilometres. Some minor route-finding farther north.

1. The trail heads north, paralleling the east face of Bellevue Hill.

2. Several kilometres along, look for a few cairns steering you left onto a fainter trail.

3. Continue north for 3.5 km in total, eventually reaching a trail sign.

4. Return the same way you came in or continue exploring (see 128 for the Horseshoe Basin Trail or 136 for Bellevue Hill). Both extensions will require lots of extra time, energy and knee cartilage!

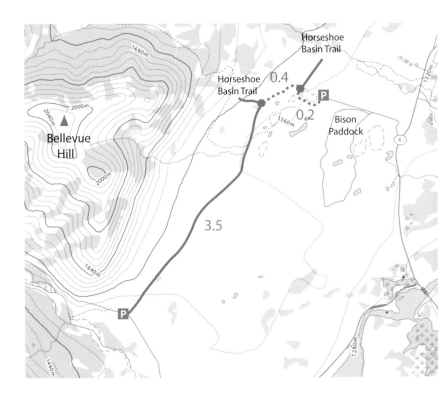

TOP: *The scariest trailhead in the Rockies! Photo Rafal Kazmierczak*

BOTTOM: *Great family hike with good views of Vimy Peak throughout.*

2 Crandell Lake

Short, easy, pleasant and scenic – good bang for your buck!

DISTANCE 3.4 KM RETURN + 1 KM AROUND THE LAKE

HEIGHT GAIN 130 M

EASY

FIRST WEEKEND OF MAY TO NOVEMBER

START: Drive 8.1 km along Red Rock Parkway and turn left at the Crandell Lake sign. Follow the signs for 0.9 km to a small parking area, where the trail begins.

DIFFICULTY: Good trail all the way to the lake. Little to no trail around the lake.

1. Follow the trail up varied terrain for 1.5 km to a trail sign. Turn left at the sign and walk 200 m to the lake. Note that as of 2021 the Crandell Lake campground was closed but may reopen in the future. Return the same way you came in.

2. Optional and recommended: if the water level allows (early to mid-July), walk around the lake in either direction, along the shore. There is a primitive trail on the east side a short distance from the shore if lakeshore travel is not feasible. From the

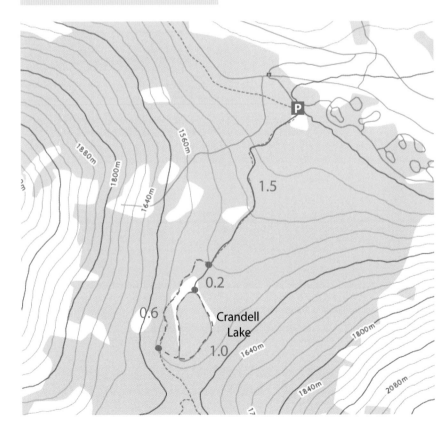

Approaching the lake. Fall colours can be very eye-catching. Photo Kari Peters

south end there are great views of Mount Galwey. If the water level is too high, you can go back to the main trail and follow it around to the south end of the lake from the west side. Return the same way you came in.

15

TOP: *Kian Nugara takes a flying leap at the lake. Photo Mark Nugara*

BOTTOM: *There is a terrific rock shelf to scramble across on the west side of the lake. Photo Mark Nugara*

3 Lost Horse Creek

The best kept secret in Waterton. A visually breathtaking jaunt up a creek, similar to Red Rock Canyon. Wear boots you can get wet and that provide good grip. Wait until mid-July.

DISTANCE 1–3 KM RETURN

HEIGHT GAIN 60 M

MODERATE WITH SOME SCRAMBLING

MID-JULY TO OCTOBER

START: Drive 11.9 km along Red Rock Parkway and park at Lost Horse Creek, on the right side of the road.

DIFFICULTY: No trail. Potentially slippery rock and deep water to wade through. Some route-finding and scrambling skills will be required farther up the creek. Use caution. Note that as time passes, dead trees from the Kenow fire may fall into the creek, making passage more difficult.

1. A snippet of a trail leads down to the creek. There is no trail once you are in the creek. Simply follow the stream on either bank, crossing where necessary. Be prepared to get your feet wet. Some sections of the creek must be waded (knee- to waist-high water). Be aware of slippery rock underfoot. Other sections will require some easy scrambling with exposure. Use caution and stop if the terrain gets too difficult for your comfort level.

2. Continue up the creek to where a subsidiary creek comes down from the left (about 45 to 90 minutes). Return the same way you came in. Note that descending the creek is often trickier than ascending it – go slowly.

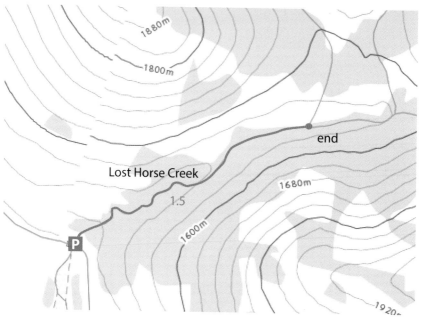

ABOVE: *One of the canyon-like features of the creek.*

OPPOSITE TOP: *One of many deep pools in the creek. The Nugara kids are happy to swim across, while the parents take the scrambling bypass route.*

OPPOSITE BOTTOM: *The terrain gets more complex upstream.*

4 Red Rock Canyon

One of the shortest and most popular hikes in Waterton. Either complete the interpretive trail above the canyon or get right in there and follow the canyon upstream (highly recommended).

DISTANCE 900 M FOR THE TRAIL

HEIGHT GAIN 25 M

HIGH POINT 1520 M

VERY EASY FOR THE INTERPRETIVE TRAIL; MODERATE FOR THE CANYON

FIRST WEEKEND OF MAY TO NOVEMBER FOR THE TRAIL; MIDSUMMER TO SEPTEMBER FOR THE CANYON

START: Drive 14 km to the end of Red Rock Parkway and park in the upper parking lot (P1) if possible, although the lower lot also works.

DIFFICULTY: Paved for the interpretive trail. No trail in the canyon. Potentially slippery rock and cold, deep water to wade through. Some route-finding and scrambling will be required farther up the creek. Use caution. Note that as time passes, dead trees from the Kenow fire may fall into the creek, making passage more difficult.

TOP: *The Red Rock Canyon trail lies on both sides of the canyon.*

BOTTOM: *The lower section of the canyon. Mount Blakiston in the background.*

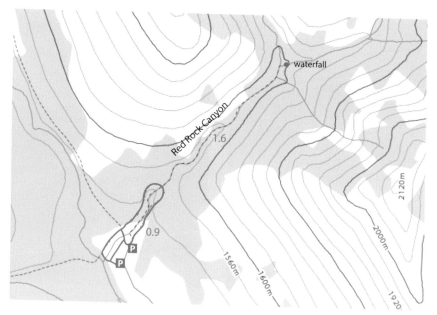

1. The interpretive trail is easy to find and easy to follow, simply making a 700 m loop around a small section of the canyon. Two bridges over the canyon provide excellent viewpoints.

2. The lower section, going down to the intersection of Red Rock Creek and Bauerman Creek, can also be easily hiked as a loop.

Going farther, up the canyon (highly recommended)

Hiking up the canyon is one of the most interesting, unique, scenic and enjoyable hikes/scrambles in the park.

> DISTANCE 2–3.2 KM RETURN
>
> HEIGHT GAIN 80 M
>
> EASY TO STRENUOUS ROCK SCRAMBLING; CHALLENGING TERRAIN FARTHER UP THE CREEK

1. From the first bridge, carefully descend into the canyon. Follow the canyon upstream as far as you like. Note that you will have to wade through sections of ankle- to waist-deep water that is very cold. Also, farther up the canyon, some sections will require easy to moderate scrambling, with exposure that may be difficult and unnerving for some, especially on return. Go only as far as your comfort level dictates and remember that descending the canyon will likely be trickier than ascending it.

2. If you go far enough, you will eventually reach a fork in the creek. Take the right fork for a short distance to check out a scenic waterfall. Return to the junction and then back to the parking lot. Travel up the other fork is not recommended.

TOP: *Easy walking at the beginning of the canyon, followed by more challenging terrain farther up (right photo).*

BOTTOM: *Red argillite eventually gives way to green argillite and other rock types.*

TOP: *Vibrant colours of rock near the beginning.*

BOTTOM: *Descending the canyon can be more challenging than ascending it, but Alpha and Mike Exner are up for it!*

5 Goat Lake

Hike to a lovely alpine lake, with terrific views along the way and plenty of options to reach a few significant summits.

DISTANCE 14 KM RETURN

HEIGHT GAIN 500 M

HIGH POINT 2017 M

STRENUOUS

SUMMER, FALL

START: Drive 14 km to the end of Red Rock Parkway and park in the upper parking lot (P1) if possible, although the lower lot also works.

DIFFICULTY: Wide, easy trail for the first 4.6 km. Narrower and steeper trail up to Goat Lake.

Hiking the scenic and easy Snowshoe Trail. Bikes are great for this trail.

1. From the upper parking lot, cross the bridge over Red Rock Canyon to Snowshoe Trail on the other side.

2. Hike or bike (preferable) 4.6 km to the signed Goat Lake junction, crossing two creeks en route. Both are usually dried up by midsummer.

3. Turn right, onto Goat Lake Trail, and hike (no bikes allowed past this point) a strenuous 2.4 km to Goat Lake, gaining almost 500 vertical metres along the way. The Goat Lake campground, at the northeast end of the lake is a perfect spot to check out the lake and have a break before returning the same way you came in or continuing to Newman Peak and/or Avion Ridge.

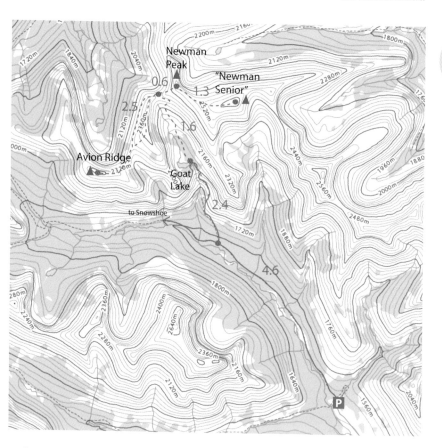

Going farther to the Avion Ridge/Newman Peak col

A wonderful extension up a scenic valley to a fantastic viewpoint.

> **DISTANCE ADD 3.2 KM RETURN**
> **HEIGHT GAIN ADD 260 M**
> **HIGH POINT 2280 M**
> **STRENUOUS LENGTH AND STEEPNESS**

1. Hike through the campground, following the signs to Avion Ridge. Note that the 1.6 km indicated by the sign is only to the col between Avion Ridge and Newman Peak and not to the summit of either.

2. The trail goes northwest, through a grassy basin, and then magically winds its way upward, through a couple of headwalls. The final stretch to the Newman Pea/Avion Ridge col veers off to the right, switchbacking up red argillite slopes. Continuing to Newman or Avion is highly recommended. Otherwise return the same way you came in.

Going farther to Newman Peak and/or "Newman Senior" (steep off-trail hiking)

Views from the summits of these peaks are terrific, especially unofficial "Newman Senior." Reaching the top of both summits makes for a relatively long and very strenuous trip, but the reward is great, especially on a bluebird day.

DISTANCE ADD 1.2–4.2 KM RETURN

HEIGHT GAIN ADD 200–360 M FROM
THE COL

HIGH POINTS 2515 M FOR NEWMAN,
2640 M FOR "NEWMAN SENIOR"

VERY STRENUOUS LENGTH AND
STEEPNESS

1. From the col, turn northeast and make your way up to the summit of Newman Peak, about 200 vertical metres above. Return the same way you came in if "Newman Senior" is not on the agenda.

2. Surprisingly, the summit of Newman Peak is not the highest point of the ridge. That honour goes to an unnamed point about 1.3 km farther east (and with a height gain of 160 vertical metres), unofficially called "Newman Senior." If you have the time and energy, this summit does provide the best view of the day. On return, if you don't mind a little side-sloping to the Avion/Newman col or trail below, it is not necessary to reascend Newman Peak.

Going farther to Avion Ridge (optional minor scrambling and off-trail hiking)

Lower than Newman Peak and "Newman Senior" but still offering a magnificent summit view due to its westerly location. Options to do a short hike (ridge route), or go to the true summit, or both!

DISTANCE ADD 5 KM RETURN FOR THE
SUMMIT OR 2 KM RETURN FOR THE
RIDGE ROUTE

HEIGHT GAIN ADD 160–240 M FROM THE
COL

HIGH POINTS 2440 M FOR AVION, 2450
M FOR THE RIDGE ROUTE

VERY STRENUOUS LENGTH AND
STEEPNESS

1. **Direct route to the summit**: from the Avion/Newman col, follow the trail south, around the right-hand side of a subsidiary peak, to the col between the true summit and the subsidiary peak, and then onto the high point of the ridge, about 2.5 km from the Newman/Avion col. Return the same way you came in.

2. **Optional ridge route** (highly recommended): from the Avion/Newman col simply follow the ridge southwest, then south to the high point about 1 km away. Either return the same way you came in or continue to the summit of Avion Ridge (again, highly recommended).

TOP: *The exciting Goat Lake Trail. Photo Dinah Kruze*

BOTTOM: *Goat Lake is superbly backdropped by the striking east face of Avion Ridge. Photo Matthew Clay*

TOP: *Looking up the valley to the Avion/Newman col at the left. Newman Peak at the centre.*

BOTTOM: *The trail neatly winds its way up through several rock bands.*

TOP: *Heading up towards the col. Photo Bob Spirko*

BOTTOM: *Just above the Newman/Avion col, the route to Newman is obvious. "Newman Senior" lies to the right. Photo Dinah Kruze*

TOP: *If a 3.3 kg, 9-year-old chihuahua named Nala can make it to the summit of Newman Peak, so can you! Photo Rafal Kazmierczak*

BOTTOM: *Hiking up to the highest summit of the day, "Newman Senior." Photo Stephen Hui*

TOP: *The reason why "Newman Senior" offers the best view.*

MIDDLE: *Part of the hike to the summit of a larch-lined Avion Ridge. Late September, early October trips are highly recommended. Photo Stephen Hui*

BOTTOM: *Typical terrain for the ridge route. Summit at the left.*

6 Sage Pass

One of the longer and more remote hikes in the park. Going farther to Kishinena Peak, or "Sage Pass Peak," offers some of the more unique views in the park.

DISTANCE 25.8 KM RETURN

HEIGHT GAIN 630 M

HIGH POINT 2131 M

STRENUOUS LENGTH

SUMMER, FALL

START: Drive 14 km to the end of Red Rock Parkway and park in the upper parking lot (P1) if possible, although the lower lot also works.

DIFFICULTY: Varied terrain on generally easy, signed trails. Biking the first 8.5 km is strongly recommended (make lots of noise, as bears frequent this area).

1. From the upper parking lot, cross the bridge over Red Rock Canyon to Snowshoe Trail on the other side.

2. Hike or bike 8.5 km to the Snowshoe campground. Leave your bike here.

3. Turn left onto Twin Lakes Trail and hike 3 km to the Sage Pass junction, just before the upper Twin Lake (the 700 m side trip to see the upper Twin Lake is worthwhile).

4. Turn right, onto the Sage Pass trail and hike 1.5 km up to the signed Sage Pass. The pass is mostly treed, and therefore continuing up towards Kishinena Peak, or "Sage Pass Peak," is highly recommended. If neither is on the agenda, you can get a better view by gaining some elevation to the northwest. Return the same way you came in.

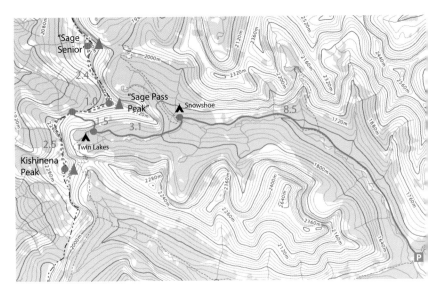

TOP: *A typical view during the bikeable section of Snowshoe Trail.*

BOTTOM: *Narrower but a great trail for the non-bikeable section. The east face of Kishinena Peak looks quite impressive and is a moderate scramble (not described here).*

TOP: *View of Kishinena Peak from just above Sage Pass.*

BOTTOM: *Optional side trip to the upper Twin Lake.*

Going farther to Kishinena Peak

Having already negotiated 12.9 km of terrain, many parties will opt to continue to the nearby summit of Kishinena Peak. Amazing views from another personal favourite!

> DISTANCE 5 KM RETURN FROM SAGE PASS
>
> HEIGHT GAIN ADD 300 M
>
> HIGH POINT 2436 M (NOTE: this route goes to the highest point on this ridge. Some maps incorrectly identify Kishinena Peak as the lower summit to the south of the highest point.)
>
> VERY STRENUOUS LENGTH AND STEEPNESS

1. From Sage Pass, hike southwest and then south-southeast to the summit. Trails are faint to non-existent, but the route is obvious. Enjoy a magnificent summit panorama from both closely spaced summit cairns and then return the same way you came in.

Going farther to "Sage Pass Peak"

Easier and shorter than going to Kishinena Peak, but still boasting wonderful views.

> DISTANCE 2 KM RETURN FROM SAGE PASS
>
> HEIGHT GAIN ADD 149 M
>
> HIGH POINT 2280 M
>
> VERY STRENUOUS LENGTH

TOP: *From near the first high point above Sage Pass, the route up Kishinena (right side of the photo) is obvious.*

BOTTOM: *More great scenery on the way to the summit. Snow can linger well into July in this area.*

TOP: *As fine a summit view as one could hope for.*

BOTTOM: *The Twin Lakes look great from above.*

1. From Sage Pass, leave the trail and turn right (east-northeast), hiking up through forest towards the ridge. The trees soon thin and the route up is obvious. Follow the ridge to the summit, enjoying improving views of the Twin Lakes, the entire west side of Waterton, the red-tinged peaks of The Castle East and mountains of the north part of Glacier National Park. Return the same way you came in or continue to "Sage Senior."

TOP: *A small section of the fantastic summit view.*

BOTTOM: *The route to "Sage Senior" is obvious, easy and remarkably scenic.*

Going farther to "Sage Senior"

The ultimate extension. Fun ridge-walking and impressive views throughout.

> DISTANCE 4.8 KM RETURN FROM "SAGE PASS PEAK"
>
> HEIGHT GAIN ADD 280 M (INCLUDES REASCENDING "SAGE PASS PEAK")
>
> HIGH POINT 2430 M
>
> VERY STRENUOUS LENGTH

1. From "Sage Pass Peak," follow the easy ridge in a northwest direction down to a col and then up towards the summit. The first summit sports an arguably better view than the true summit a short distance away. Visit both and then return the same way you came in. Continuing northwest along the ridge is certainly feasible but turns a very long day into a crazy long day!

TOP: *The fascinating summit block of "Senior." The route stays well to the left, on very easy terrain.*

BOTTOM: *The excellent view to the south from near the summit includes Sage Pass Peak, Kishinena Peak, a few small lakes and much more.*

7 Blakiston Falls

Short hike to a scenic waterfall.

DISTANCE 2 KM RETURN

HEIGHT GAIN 15 M

EASY

FIRST WEEKEND OF MAY TO NOVEMBER

START: Drive 14 km to the end of Red Rock Parkway and park in the lower parking lot (P2) if possible, although the upper also works.

DIFFICULTY: Good, maintained trail, mostly flat, with a few gentle hills.

For map, see page 43, Blakiston Valley.

1. From either parking lot, hike to the bridges that cross Red Rock Canyon and Bauerman Creek. Cross both and follow the signed trail for 1 km to the Blakiston Falls viewpoint platforms. Return the same way you came in or continue the trip up the valley.

Going farther up Blakiston Creek

Highly recommended extension to see an amazing red argillite creek bed.

DISTANCE ADD 2.4 KM RETURN

HEIGHT GAIN ADD 30 M

EASY

1. Continue hiking west on the trail paralleling Blakiston Creek for about 15–20

Blakiston Falls Trail in 2020, three years after the Kenow fire.

minutes, to a short but incredibly scenic
section of the creek where red argillite
rock has been exposed. Explore and then
return the same way you came in or continue up the valley for as long as desired
(see next trip).

ABOVE: *A smaller waterfall is encountered on the way to the red argillite section.*

OPPOSITE: *Approaching Blakiston Falls and the viewing platforms.*

TOP: *The red argillite section. One of my favourite spots in the entire park.*

BOTTOM: *Lots of opportunities here for long-exposure photos.*

8 Blakiston Valley

Very long hike alongside Blakiston Creek, and the launch point for ascents of Mount Bauerman, Kishinena Peak or Lone Mountain.

DISTANCE 20.2 KM RETURN

HEIGHT GAIN 450 M

HIGH POINT 1920

STRENUOUS LENGTH

FIRST WEEKEND OF MAY TO NOVEMBER

START: Drive 14 km to the end of Red Rock Parkway and park in the lower lot (P2) if possible, although the upper lot also works.

DIFFICULTY: Good, maintained trail with a few hills, but steeper with lots of elevation gain near the end.

1. From either parking lot, hike to the bridges that cross Red Rock Canyon and Bauerman Creek. Cross both and follow the signed trail for 1 km to Blakiston Falls.

2. From Blakiston Falls, continue hiking up the valley on a good trail, enjoying good views of Mount Blakiston on the left side of the valley and Anderson Peak on the right side. Hike as far up the valley as desired, returning the same way you came in when satiated. The Blakiston Creek trail is about 10 km in length and ends at a 3-way, signed junction. If you make it to this junction, consider an ascent of Mount Bauerman, Lone Mountain or Kishinena Peak. Note that these ascents make for a long day with tons of hiking, but offer excellent views. Also note that staying at one of the nearby campgrounds (Lone Lake or Twin Lakes) is a great option. Book ahead.

Going farther to Mount Bauerman

An outstanding viewpoint that's worth the price of 28 km of very strenuous hiking.

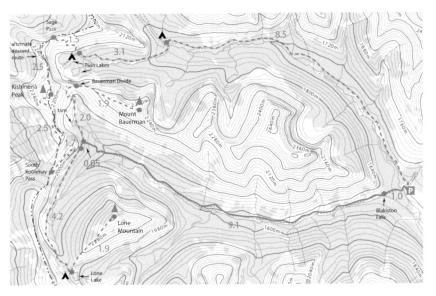

43

TOP: *Early morning in the valley.*

BOTTOM: *Approaching the end of the Blakiston Creek trail. Kishinena Peak is to the right.*

TOP: *Karen, Jill and Ryan Alston hike back to Red Rock Canyon. Waterton's highest peak, Mount Blakiston, lines the south side of the valley.*

BOTTOM: *The shallow tarn is worth a quick visit en route. Note the Bauerman Divide (pass) near the right.*

DISTANCE ADD 7.8 KM RETURN FROM THE 3-WAY JUNCTION

HEIGHT GAIN ADD 490 M FROM THE 3-WAY JUNCTION

HIGH POINT 2409 M

VERY STRENUOUS LENGTH AND STEEPNESS

1. Hike to the end of the valley (9.1 km from Blakiston Falls) and turn right at the signed intersection towards Twin Lakes.

2. Hike approximately 2 km, passing a scenic shallow tarn on the way, to the Bauerman Divide (pass) between Kishinena Peak and Mount Bauerman. If you start losing elevation towards Twin Lakes, you have gone a little too far.

TOP: *Approaching the false summit of Bauerman, near the right. You'll reach the true summit shortly after.*

BOTTOM: *Karen Alston and son Ryan at the windy summit of Mount Bauerman, having just completed the awesome Anderson-Lost-Kootenai Brown-Bauerman traverse.*

3. From the pass, turn right (east) and grind your way up to the summit of Mount Bauerman, gaining 320 metres of elevation over 1.9 horizontal kilometres. The first section is through light forest and there are various trails to follow. Once out of the trees, it's an easy and scenic hike to the summit. Return the same way you came in. Alternative routes down are possible but not recommended. Refer to *More Scrambles in the Canadian Rockies, 3rd Edition* for more information. If you really want to experience the area, once down at the pass and back on the trail, turn north towards Twin Lakes and hike out via the Tamarack, Twin Lakes and Snowshoe trails, ending right back where you started – a very, very long day but with incredible scenery throughout!

TOP: *On return, the view of the valley you just ascended is one of the highlights of the trip.*

BOTTOM: *The view to the west that you won't see if you call it quits at South Kootenay Pass.*

TOP: *Amazing terrain en route to Kishinena Peak.*

BOTTOM: *There is no direct route to the summit of Kishinena. You have to go around at the left side.*

Going farther to South Kootenay Pass and Kishinena Peak

A more challenging route to Kishinena Peak than that from Sage Pass, but wonderfully scenic and very interesting.

DISTANCE ADD 9.1 KM RETURN FROM THE 3-WAY JUNCTION

HEIGHT GAIN ADD 530 M FROM THE 3-WAY JUNCTION

HIGH POINT 2436 M
(NOTE: This route goes to the highest point on this ridge. Some maps incorrectly identify Kishinena Peak as the lower summit to the south of the high point.)

VERY STRENUOUS LENGTH AND STEEPNESS

1. Hike to the end of the valley (9.1 km from Blakiston Falls), and at the signed junction turn left, towards Lone Lake.

2. In 50 m turn right, onto the South Kootenay Pass trail.

3. The SKP trail is 1.7 km long and switchbacks up to a completely treed pass. There are no views at all from here.

4. Remedy this shortcoming by turning north and hiking up through light forest towards Kishinena Peak. Staying close to the ridge offers the best views, and above treeline the view opens up fully. You can turn around at any point and return the same way you came in.

5. Going all the way to the summit of Kishinena Peak requires some tenacity and also an elevation loss to the left to make the final push. Fortunately the route is obvious. Simply follow the ridge north until the summit block is close.

6. A nearly vertical wall of rock guards the summit but is easily circumvented by losing a little elevation to the left. Go around the difficulties and resume travel towards the top.

7. Once heading to the summit, it is best to find a route through the trees, as opposed to staying close to the exposed ridge. Enjoy the magnificent summit panorama and then return the same way you came in or make an adventurous loop route as described next.

8. Returning via Sage Pass, Twin Lakes Trail and Snowshoe Trail are only slightly longer than returning the same way you came, and they are far more interesting. The only real challenge is to find the Sage Pass trail, as there is no trail to get there. However, the location of the pass is obvious.

9. Descend the northwest ridge of Kishinena, eventually turning northeast towards Sage Pass. The pass is the obvious low point, but finding the trail may take a little searching. Once on the trail, follow it down to Twin Lakes Trail and turn left (east). Twin Lakes Trail leads to the Snowshoe campground and Snowshoe Trail, which will take you back to Red Rock Canyon in 7.8 km.

Going farther to Lone Lake and Lone Mountain

If you have visited the summit of Bauerman and/or Kishinena, Lone Mountain is a terrific alternative. Once again, it's a very long and strenuous day unless you are already camped at Lone Lake.

DISTANCE ADD 12.2 KM RETURN FROM THE 3-WAY JUNCTION

HEIGHT GAIN ADD 500 M FROM THE 3-WAY JUNCTION

HIGH POINT 2420 M

VERY STRENUOUS LENGTH AND STEEPNESS

TOP: *Hiking through lush meadows and below the Continental Divide, towards Lone Lake.*

BOTTOM: *Ryan Alston and Alan Wiley hike the gentle, red argillite slopes of Lone Mountain. Photo Jill Alston*

Ryan and Jill Alston are all smiles atop this rarely ascended peak. Photo Reggie Williams

1. Hike to the end of the valley (9.1 km from Blakiston Falls) to the signed junction and turn left, towards Lone Lake.

2. Hike 4.2 km to Lone Lake and the campground. Locate the campground hanging posts for food. It's the best place to start the ascent.

3. Turn north and start hiking upward through light forest, trending a little to the left. This first part it is steepest section of the ascent.

4. As you gain elevation the grade lessens and the trees thin. Stay close to the ridge for the best views. It should take about 45 minutes to reach the summit.

5. Take a well-deserved and long break (if doing this route as a day trip), and then return the same way you came in. DO NOT attempt any shortcut routes down the mountain. There are unseen rock bands and thick foliage that will stop progress.

AKAMINA PARKWAY

Akamina Parkway starts just before the townsite, 7.6 km from the park gate. Although the actual drive is not as scenic as Red Rock Parkway, Akamina Parkway is the launching point for three of the most scenic trips in Waterton: Lineham Ridge, Akamina Ridge and Carthew–Alderson. Again, a reminder that the final 2.5 km of the road is closed to motor vehicles from November until the first weekend of May, though walking, biking, skiing and snowshoeing are permitted.

Fall colours above Forum Lake en route to Akamina Ridge.

9 Crandell Lake

The shortest route to Crandell Lake that is also accessible year-round. Snowshoes, skis or winter traction devices will be useful for winter trips.

DISTANCE 2.8 KM RETURN +1 KM
    AROUND THE LAKE
HEIGHT GAIN 180 M
HIGH POINT 1575 M
EASY
YEAR-ROUND

START: Drive 6.7 km along Akamina Parkway and park at the signed trailhead for Crandell Lake.

DIFFICULTY: Good trail all the way to the lake. Moderate grade with a few steeper sections. Little to no trail around the lake.

1. From the trailhead, hike 800 m up to a junction.

2. Turn left and hike 400 m, losing elevation, to another junction and a hiking/no biking trail sign.

3. Turn right and reach the south end of the lake in 200 m. This trail can be quite overgrown at times. Great views of Mount Galwey to the north. Return the same way you came in.

4. Optional and recommended: if the water level is low enough, hike around the lake in either direction along the shore. There is a

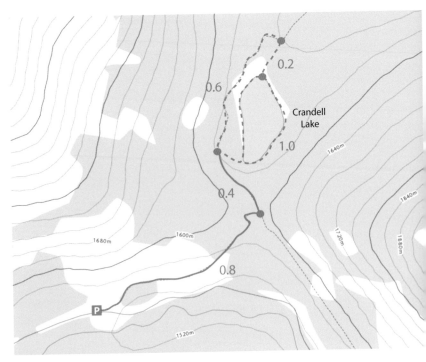

Kian Nugara takes note of a distinctively bent tree alongside the trail.

TOP: *Father and son descend the trail to Crandell Lake, seen at the right. The summit in front is the east peak of Ruby Ridge, a fantastic trip described on page 60.*

BOTTOM: *Early-season view from the south side of the lake.*

campground at the north end (closed in 2021) and a small picnic area. If the water is too high you can get around to the north side of the lake by returning to the main trail and following it around to the north.

10 Lineham Falls

A pleasant and easy hike to a beautiful 100 m waterfall.

DISTANCE 9.2 KM RETURN

HEIGHT GAIN 350 M

HIGH POINT 1975 M

MODERATE

SUMMER, FALL

START: Drive 9.1 km along Akamina Parkway and park at the signed trailhead for Lineham.

DIFFICULTY: Good trail to a point several hundred metres before the falls. Faint to no trail to get all the way to the base of the falls.

1. Hike the Lineham Creek Falls trail as it skirts the lower slopes of Ruby Ridge and later Mount Blakiston.

2. About 45–55 minutes along, cross an open creek (sometimes dried up). Don't take the faint right fork that goes up the creek towards Mount Blakiston.

3. Shortly after the creek crossing there is a small but scenic waterfall to check out on the left side. A faint trail takes you there in less than a minute. Then return to the main trail.

4. Continue on the trail to the TRAIL ENDS sign, where you will get an excellent view

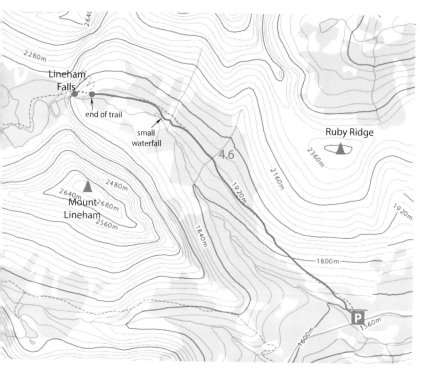

TOP: *The impressive northeast face of Mount Lineham is one of the highlights early in the hike.*

BOTTOM: *The small but beautiful waterfall after the creek crossing.*

TOP: *Lineham Falls from the end of the trail.*

BOTTOM: *The rewards of an early-season trip are increased water flow and remaining snow scenery.*

of Lineham Falls and the steep walls of mounts Lineham and Blakiston. Return the same way you came in.

5. Optional and recommended: if desired, continue on faint trails all the way to the falls. There are a few steep sections of scree to contend with. Great views and lots of room for exploration, but be careful around the falls. Return the same way you came in.

11 Ruby Ridge

Very steep, off-trail hike/scramble to an excellent viewpoint in the shadow of Waterton's highest peak, Mount Blakiston.

DISTANCE 6 KM RETURN

HEIGHT GAIN 965 M

HIGH POINT 2430 M

VERY STRENUOUS STEEPNESS

LATE SPRING, SUMMER, FALL

START: Drive 9.1 km along Akamina Parkway and park at the signed trailhead for Lineham.

DIFFICULTY: Good trail to start, followed by very steep and trail-less travel up scree and rubble to the summit.

1. Hike the Lineham Falls trail for about 1.7 km to a point just before the trail heads into the trees.

2. Turn upslope (right) and away you go. The terrain is relentlessly steep and you will know within minutes if it is to your liking or not. Slog your way to the summit, heading generally northeast, picking the line of least resistance. There is no formal trail.

3. Take in the excellent view of Mount Blakiston with Ruby Lake below it, and then either return the same way you came in or continue to the east peak (highly recommended).

Going farther to the east peak

Arguably the best part of trip, featuring a glut of great red argillite scenery.

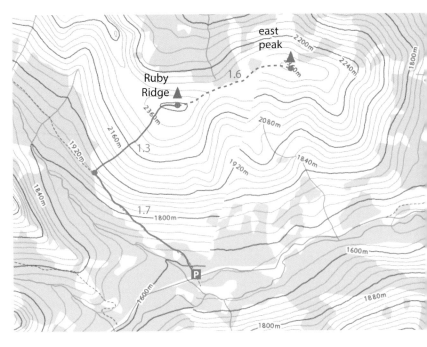

TOP: *Bob and Ray grind their way up the steep, trail-less slopes. If an hour or two of this kind of terrain doesn't look appealing, this may not be the trip for you. Photo Dinah Kruze*

BOTTOM: *The view to the west may help keep your mind off the tedium of the ascent. Still very snowy in mid-March.*

TOP: *An "in your face" view of Mount Blakiston and Ruby Lake.*

BOTTOM: *Ray and Dinah start down Ruby's east ridge towards the east peak. Photo Bob Spirko*

OPPOSITE: *Serge Massad and Zosia Zgolak explore the colourful east peak. Photo Sonny Bou*

DISTANCE 3.2 KM RETURN

**HEIGHT GAIN ADD 270 M (INCLUDES THE
RETURN TRIP)**

HIGH POINT 2390 M

STRENUOUS STEEPNESS

1. From the summit, simply head east, descending small rock bands of spectacular red argillite. Small detours on either side of the ridge (but mostly the left side) and good route-finding will be required to discover the easiest route down.

2. Descend to the col between the peaks and then hike easily up to the summit of the east peak. Return the same way you came in. There are more-direct routes down, but all involve very steep terrain, route-finding and bushwhacking – not recommended.

12 Rowe Lakes

One decent lake and two awesome lakes in beautiful surroundings. Great during larch season.

DISTANCE 8.2 KM RETURN FOR THE LOWER LAKE, 12.8 KM RETURN FOR THE UPPER LAKES

HEIGHT GAIN 350 M FOR THE LOWER LAKE, 575 M FOR THE UPPER LAKES

HIGH POINT 2175 M

MODERATE FOR LOWER LAKE, STRENUOUS FOR UPPER LAKES

SUMMER, EARLY FALL

START: Drive 10.4 km along Akamina Parkway and park at the signed trailhead for Rowe/Tamarack.

DIFFICULTY: Good, maintained trail to all lakes. Gentle grade for Lower Lake, much steeper for Upper Lakes. The trail to Upper Lakes holds snow well into July sometimes.

1. Hike 3.9 km to the first junction. A few hundred metres up the trail (from the parking lot) there are two opportunities to descend to the left to check out Rowe Creek flowing down the red argillite rock.

2. At the 3.9 km mark, turn left to the Lower Lake (the "decent" one). Return to the junction.

3. Continue along the Rowe Lakes trail, eventually arriving at an open area called Rowe Meadows. Cross a creek on a footbridge and arrive at another trail sign. Turn left towards Upper Rowe Lake.

4. Hike the steep, switchbacking trail up to the lakes (the "awesome" ones).

5. There are two lakes atop the headwall, connected by a pretty stream. Explore the shores of each as desired and then return the same way you came in.

One of the first opportunities to check out the colourful creek, only minutes from the parking lot. Photo Marko Stavric

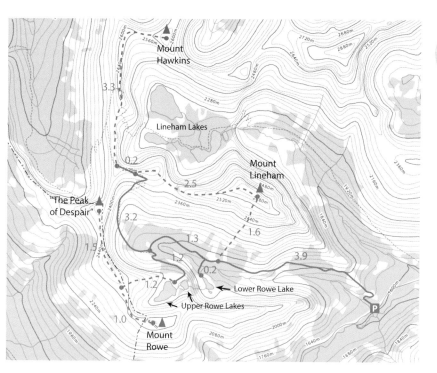

At the south side of the highest and biggest Upper Rowe Lake.

Going farther to Mount Rowe

Highly enjoyable ascent to an outstanding viewpoint.

DISTANCE 4.4 KM RETURN

HEIGHT GAIN ADD 360 M

HIGH POINT 2469 M

STRENUOUS STEEPNESS AND LENGTH

1. From the higher Upper Lake, hike up the wide, larch-filled ridge that starts at the north end of the lake. Gain the ridge northwest of Mount Rowe. Be cautious on snow that remains below the ridge.

2. Hike/scramble southeast, then east to the summit of Mount Rowe. Return the same way you came in or if time permits do the extension to GR133383, "The Peak of Despair."

TOP: *The colourful drainage that connects the highest Upper Lake to the slightly lower Upper Lake.*

BOTTOM: *In the fall, the slightly lower Upper Lake can shrink to the size of a big puddle, but can still produce awesome reflections. Photo Dave McMurray*

TOP: *The wide ridge that grants an excellent view of the lakes.*

BOTTOM: *Upon reaching the ridge, it's a beautiful stroll to the summit of Mount Rowe at the right. Photo Mark Nugara*

Going farther to GR133383, "The Peak of Despair"

Higher than Mount Rowe and boasting equally, if not more, impressive views.

DISTANCE 2.5 KM ONE WAY FROM THE
SUMMIT OF MOUNT ROWE

HEIGHT GAIN ADD 100 M FROM THE
SUMMIT OF MOUNT ROWE

HIGH POINT 2518 M

STRENUOUS LENGTH

1. From the summit of Rowe, hike back along the west and northwest ridges and keep going. A red subsidiary summit is reached first and then continue down and then up to the high point at GR133383 – unofficially nicknamed "The Peak of Despair" by Dave McMurray because of a failed and desperate attempt we made to get down to the col east of The Peak. Return the same way you came in. Continuing along the ridge towards Mount Festubert is also an option (see *More Scrambles* for details).

TOP: *Staying near the ridge on the way to the first high point grants the best views.*

MIDDLE: *Dave McMurray takes the last few steps to the summit of "The Peak of Despair."*

BOTTOM: *The east side of the ridge is home to swaths of brilliant red argillite.*

OPPOSITE: *Dave McMurray at the summit of Rowe.*

69

13 Lineham Ridge

Like Akamina Ridge, simply one of the best viewpoints in Waterton.

DISTANCE 17.2 KM RETURN

HEIGHT GAIN 950 M

HIGH POINT 2560 M

STRENUOUS

SUMMER, EARLY FALL

START: Drive 10.4 km along Akamina Parkway and park at the signed trailhead for Rowe/Tamarack.

DIFFICULTY: Good, easy trail to Rowe Meadows. Steeper and a little more challenging up to Lineham Ridge, on red argillite scree. Steep snow patches may linger well into July and can be difficult to get past.

For map, see page 64, Rowe Lakes.

1. Hike 3.9 km to the first junction. A few hundred metres up the trail (from the parking lot) there are two opportunities to descend to the left to check out Rowe Creek flowing down red argillite rock.

2. Optional: turn left at the 3.9 km mark to visit Lower Rowe Lake, 200 m away. Otherwise, continue going straight, eventually arriving at an open area called Rowe Meadows. Cross a creek on a footbridge and arrive at another trail sign. Turn right towards Lineham Ridge.

3. Hike 3.3 km up and across the basin to the high point of Lineham Ridge and a fantastic view of the Lineham Lakes. Note that the trail goes under and past the high point of Lineham Ridge before turning almost 180° and then going west and up to the high point. Enjoy the spectacular view, then return the same way you came in or consider one or both of the highly recommended extensions.

Going farther, north along Lineham Ridge

DISTANCE VARIABLE TO 6.6 KM RETURN

HEIGHT GAIN VARIABLE TO 470 M

HIGH POINT 2560 TO 2685 M

STRENUOUS TO VERY STRENUOUS

LENGTH AND STEEPNESS

Five brave souls venture up to Rowe Meadows in late May. The Lineham Ridge trail goes from left to right, above treeline. The summit of Lineham Ridge is at the centre.

TOP: *The excellent Lineham Ridge trail is easy to follow when snow-free. Photo Daniel Yang*

MIDDLE: *Approaching the point where the trail turns sharply, with Mount Lineham in the background. Photo Bob Spirko*

BOTTOM: *The stunning Lineham Lakes, below mounts Lineham (right) and Blakiston (left). Photo Mark Nugara*

1. For even better views of the Lineham Lakes and the Blakiston Horseshoe (the ring of mountains around the lakes), follow the ridge going north (not on the Tamarack trail below the ridge). There is no trail, but the terrain is easy to negotiate. Go as far as time, energy and your comfort level dictate. Fit and motivated parties could make it all the way to the red-tinged summit of Mount Hawkins. Return the same way you came in. Do not attempt any alternative descent routes.

Going farther to Mount Lineham

> **DISTANCE ADD 2.7 KM ONE WAY TO THE SUMMIT**
> **HEIGHT GAIN ADD 320 M**
> **HIGH POINT 2728 M**
> **VERY STRENUOUS:** length and steepness

1. From the high point of Lineham Ridge, simply follow the ridge east all the way to the summit of Mount Lineham. Although you can stay on the trail for the first part, the most scenic route stays near the ridge. From the low point, a decent trail leads to the summit, but again the best views are served up from the ridge. Minor scrambling may be required but is always avoidable.

2. The summit view is excellent, its only shortcoming the lack of views of the Lineham Lakes. Return the same way you came in. There is a shortcut that goes straight down a wide scree/rubble gully on the south face. However, this option is recommended only for experienced parties who are comfortable on very steep, loose terrain and have good route-finding abilities. Near the bottom of the gully, a stint of annoying bushwhacking takes you back to the Rowe Lakes trail.

If you go far enough, you get to see the wild variety of colours on the ridge. Photo Mark Nugara

TOP: *Starting the scenic trek to Mount Lineham (right). Photo Mark Nugara*

MIDDLE: *Last look at the Lineham Lakes before you reach the summit.*

BOTTOM: *Looking down the alternative descent route. Don't underestimate it. It's very steep, with hidden rock bands.*

14 Forum Lake

A small but scenic waterfall, followed by a small but scenic lake, with the highly recommended option to continue to Akamina Ridge, high above the lake.

DISTANCE 8.8 KM RETURN

HEIGHT GAIN 350 M

HIGH POINT 1990 M

MODERATE

SUMMER, EARLY FALL

START: Drive 14.8 km along Akamina Parkway and park at the signed trailhead for Akamina Pass.

DIFFICULTY: Easy, signed trail to Akamina Pass. Steeper but well-marked trail to Forum Lake. More challenging terrain to Akamina Ridge, with a few sections of easy scrambling. Biking to Akamina Pass is permitted.

1. Hike or bike 1.5 km to Akamina Pass. From here on in you will be in Akamina–Kishinena Provincial Park, BC.

2. Continue down the other side of the pass for 700 m and turn left onto the Forum Falls/Lake trail. Bikes are not allowed on this part of the trail.

3. The Forum Falls turnoff is only 200 m along the trail and well worth a short side trip.

4. Return to the Forum Lake trail and continue up it for another 1.8 km to the lake. Use the boardwalks, where they appear, to help protect this fragile environment.

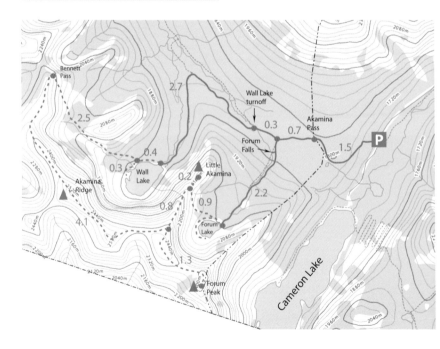

5. Enjoy the excellent scenery around the lake before returning the same way you came in or continue on to Akamina Ridge. It is possible to hike counterclockwise around to the west and south sides of Forum Lake, but a full circumnavigation is difficult because of steep, rocky terrain on the east side.

Going farther to Akamina Ridge

One of the finest ridgewalks and viewpoints in the park. A must-do trip if you are up for some steep, trail-less travel and easy rock scrambling.

DISTANCE ADD 12.4 KM IN TOTAL (BACK TO PARKING LOT)

HEIGHT GAIN ADD 625 M

HIGH POINT 2565 M

VERY STRENUOUS STEEPNESS AND LENGTH

TOP: *Forum Falls.*

BOTTOM: *Dinah Kruze hikes the boardwalks. Photo Bob Spirko*

TOP: *Forum Lake.*

BOTTOM: *The trail up to the ridge, northwest of the lake.*

1. From the shores of Forum Lake an obvious, signed trail heads west, skirting the north side of the lake, and then goes steeply up to the ridge northwest of the lake.

2. Upon reaching the ridge, turn southwest (left) and follow it up towards the next high point. There are trails that guide you past most of the rock scrambling, but a few easy moves of scrambling will be required. It is also possible to scramble directly up the ridge here. **Note:** before you venture up this ridge, check out the description for "Little Akamina" starting on page 78.

3. Approaching the high point, the trail veers off to the right. Note that this high point sits between the summits of Forum Peak to the east and Akamina Ridge to the west. See next description for Forum Peak.

4. For Akamina Ridge, follow the ridge west, over another high point, and then on to the summit of the ridge. Views throughout this ridgewalk are remarkable. The ridge is very close to the Canada/U.S. border, so everything you see to the south lies in Glacier National Park, Montana.

5. The best way to return is via Bennett Pass to the west and then Wall Lake as follows. Continue along the ridge in a northwest direction and then north and down towards Bennett Pass (the col northwest of the summit).

6. Just before reaching the low point, the trail turns right (east) and drops down towards Wall Lake, several kilometres away.

7. Once on the Wall Lake trail, follow it back down to the main trail. Turn right and hike back up to Akamina Pass and then down to the parking lot.

TOP: *Almost at the upper ridge, where the panorama really opens up.*

BOTTOM: *Heading down the alternative descent route via Bennett Pass. Note that the trail goes around the left side of the bump ahead and is also just visible in the foliage, far below at the right. Photo Bob Spirko*

Approaching Wall Lake on return.

Going farther to Forum Peak

A shorter alternative to the Akamina summit, with an outstanding view of Cameron Lake and peaks in Glacier National Park.

DISTANCE ADD 6 KM RETURN FROM
FORUM LAKE

HEIGHT GAIN ADD 500 M FROM FORUM
LAKE

HIGH POINT 2460 M

VERY STRENUOUS STEEPNESS AND
LENGTH

1. From the shores of Forum Lake an obvious, signed trail heads west, skirting the north side of the lake, and then goes steeply up to the ridge northwest of the lake.

2. Upon reaching the ridge, turn southwest (left) and follow it up towards the next high point. There are trails that guide you past most of the rock scrambling, but a few easy moves of scrambling will be required. It is also possible to scramble directly up the ridge here.

3. Approaching the high point, the trail veers off to the right, but you will want to go straight up or up and slightly to the left. The high point is actually higher than Forum Peak, so it is worth a visit.

4. From the high point descend easy slopes to the east and then up to Forum Peak. There are several large cairns and viewpoints, all of them worth checking out. Return the same way you came in.

Going farther to "Little Akamina"

If the long trip to Akamina Ridge or Forum Peak is not in the cards, this minor high point offers an excellent view of both Forum and Wall lakes.

TOP: *Heading to Forum Peak in front. Staying near the ridge on the left grants good views of Forum Lake.*

MIDDLE: *Fantastic view of Cameron Lake.*

BOTTOM: *An equally spectacular view into Glacier National Park and an odd arrangement of rocks!*

DISTANCE ADD 2 KM RETURN FROM
FORUM LAKE

HEIGHT GAIN ADD 180 FROM FORUM
LAKE

HIGH POINT 2170 M

STRENUOUS STEEPNESS AND LENGTH

1. From the shores of Forum Lake an obvious, signed trail heads west, skirting the north side of the lake, and then goes steeply up to the ridge northwest of the lake.

2. Upon reaching the ridge, turn northeast (right) and make your way to the high point only 200 m away. It's an easier ascent than appearances dictate and involves only a few steep steps. After marvelling at the awesome view of Forum and Wall lakes, as well as other beautiful sights, return the same way you came in.

TOP: *The last stretch to the summit of "Little Akamina."*

BOTTOM: *Always a treat to see two lakes in two different valleys simultaneously.*

15 Wall Lake

The twin to Forum Lake. A pleasant hike or exhilarating bike to a beautiful lake that is surrounded by steep walls, again with the option to reach the summit of stunning Akamina Ridge.

DISTANCE 10.4 KM RETURN

HEIGHT GAIN 125 M

HIGH POINT 1800 M

MODERATE

SUMMER, EARLY FALL

START: Drive 14.8 km along Akamina Parkway and park at the signed trailhead for Akamina Pass.

DIFFICULTY: Slightly easier than Forum Lake, as less elevation gain is required. Good trail all the way to the lake. Biking the entire trail to Wall Lake is permitted. Steep ascent to Akamina Ridge is also possible from Wall Lake.

The still, crystal-clear waters of Wall Lake. Early morning is usually the best chance to get perfect lake reflections.

For map, see page 74, Forum Lake.

1. Hike or bike 1.5 km to Akamina Pass. From here on in you will be in Akamina–Kishinena Provincial Park, B.C.

2. Continue down the other side of the pass for 1 km and turn left onto the Wall Lake trail. Bikes are permitted all the way to Wall Lake. It's 2.7 km from the turnoff to the lake.

3. There are several spots where you are granted good views across the lake. It is worth it to follow the trail west for 400 m as it traverses the north side of the lake and then goes another 200 m south, around to the west side. Return the same way you came in or go back to the sign for Bennett Pass and continue to Akamina Ridge as described below.

TOP: *Much truth to the idiom "tip of the iceberg"! They sometimes persist into early July at the northwest end of Wall Lake.*

BOTTOM: *After the lake, the route goes up this beautiful valley. Large snow patches can persist well into July in this area.*

At the ridge, the red summit of Akamina Ridge above Wall Lake can be seen. Photo Matthew Hobbs

Going farther to Akamina Ridge (see Forum Lake on page 74 for more photos)

A slightly easier, though longer, route than that from Forum Lake. Lots of elevation gain – don't underestimate it.

> DISTANCE ADD 5 KM ONE WAY
> HEIGHT GAIN ADD 760 M
> HIGH POINT 2565 M
> VERY STRENUOUS STEEPNESS AND
>   LENGTH

1. From the west end of the lake, jump onto the Bennett Pass trail and follow it going west and gently up. A few kilometres along, the trail gets steeper and ascends to the northwest end of Akamina Ridge.

2. Upon reaching the ridge, turn left (south) and follow the ridge (south, then southeast) to the summit, about 2.4 km and 360 vertical metres away. On a clear day, expect outstanding views in every direction.

3. Return the same way you came in. If you are confident about your route-finding and down-climbing abilities, it is possible to return via Forum Lake. However, this route is preferable and easier in the reverse direction (as described on page 75) and therefore not recommended in the other direction.

16 Cameron Lakeshore

Enjoy the peaceful waters of Cameron Lake below impressive Mount Custer. Boat or paddle board around the lake after.

DISTANCE 3.2 KM RETURN

HEIGHT GAIN MINIMAL

VERY EASY

SPRING, SUMMER, EARLY FALL

START: Drive 16 km to Cameron Lake, at the end of Akamina Parkway.

DIFFICULTY: Mostly flat trail to the platform.

1. The trail is easily found on the west (right) side of the lake. Follow it for 1.6 km to a viewing platform. The best views of the lake will be experienced en route and not at the platform, where there are no views at all. DO NOT hike past the platform. This is prime grizzly bear habitat. Return the same way you came in and then consider renting a paddle board, paddle boat, kayak or canoe to really explore the lake.

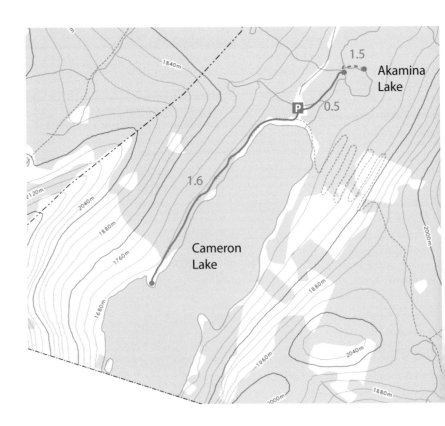

TOP: *The reward of an early morning trip to Cameron Lake can be sublime views such as this one. Photo Marko Stavric*

MIDDLE: *The reward of a winter trip to the lake can be stunning views like this. No boat needed to cross the lake but be sure it's fully frozen!*

BOTTOM: *Amelie Stavric enjoys the picturesque south end of Cameron Lake. Boat required! Photo Marko Stavric*

17 Akamina Lake

A very short and worthwhile side trip if you are already at Cameron Lake.

DISTANCE 1 KM RETURN

HEIGHT GAIN MINIMAL

VERY EASY

SUMMER, EARLY FALL

START: Drive 16 km to Cameron Lake, at the end of Akamina Parkway.

DIFFICULTY: Short, easy trail.

For map, see page 84, Cameron Lake.

1. The official trail starts between the washroom buildings on the left (east) side of the parking lot. Follow the trail for 500 m to a small platform at the lake. Before the Kenow fire, views were fairly limited from the platform, but in 2021 they were more open. If conditions warrant, you can hike southwest along the lakeshore for a more comprehensive view. Return the same way you came in.

2. Optional: if you don't mind getting your feet wet, ford the lake outlet and follow a faint animal trial along the northwest side of the lake for about 150 m. There you will be treated to an excellent view of Mount Custer, Forum Peak and Akamina Lake. Travelling farther around the lake is not recommended.

BELOW: *Akamina Lake from near the platform, before the Kenow fire. The peak above the lake, unofficially called "Carthew Minor," is a terrific scramble.*

OPPOSITE TOP: *The view from the north side of the lake, after fording the lake outlet.*

OPPOSITE BOTTOM: *Some of the wildlife at Akamina Lake.*

18 Summit Lake

Not only a beautiful lake, backdropped by several stunning mountains, but also the launching point for several of the best hikes/scrambles in the park.

DISTANCE 8.0 KM RETURN

HEIGHT GAIN 305 M

HIGH POINT 1906 M

MODERATE

SUMMER, EARLY FALL

START: Drive 16 km to Cameron Lake, at the end of Akamina Parkway.

DIFFICULTY: Good, signed trail all the way.

1. The trail is easily found on the east (left) side of the lake. Note that as of 2021 Summit Lake was not included on the sign, only Carthew and Alderson lakes. Hike along the lakeshore and then follow several very long switchbacks to a plateau, where the terrain becomes flatter.

2. Keep going as the trail gently descends to Summit Lake. The shapely peaks that backdrop the lake are Mount Custer and Chapman Peak, both in Glacier National Park, Montana. Hiking a short distance around the northeast side of the lake on the Boundary Bay trail provides additional views of the surroundings. Going around the entire lake is not recommended, because of the fragility of the terrain. Return the same way you came in or continue to Carthew Summit.

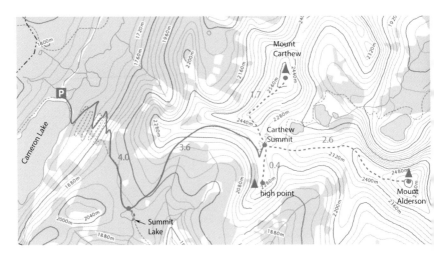

TOP: *Views from the long switchbacks are limited but more open since the Kenow fire. Forum Peak sits above Cameron Lake.*

MIDDLE: *A great view of Summit Lake. Chapman Peak (left) and Mount Custer (right) are far behind the lake, in Glacier National Park, Montana. Photo Naheer Hirji*

BOTTOM: *A minor outlier above the lake, as seen from the lake outlet.*

19 Carthew Summit

If you have made it to Summit Lake, go the extra 3.6 km to an amazing viewpoint.

DISTANCE 15.2 KM RETURN

HEIGHT GAIN 650 M

HIGH POINT 2311 M

STRENUOUS

SUMMER, EARLY FALL

START: Drive 16 km to Cameron Lake, at the end of Akamina Parkway.

DIFFICULTY: The route is largely along a red argillite scree trail. Some steep sections and minor scrambling if you go to the high point.

For map, see page 88, Summit Lake.

1. Follow the directions to Summit Lake.

2. Return to the main trail and continue following it northeastward, eventually entering an open bowl below Mount Carthew.

3. Follow the red argillite trail up to the low point between two peaks for a stunning view of Mount Alderson and many others. This is Carthew Summit.

4. Optional and highly recommended: from the low point follow the ridge south to the high point at the end. A little scrambling will be required. Fantastic views again, even better than those from the col.

Once out of the tress, the route to Carthew Summit becomes obvious. The summit is the low col. The higher point at the far right can be easily attained and is highly recommended. Photo Steve Patitsas

TOP: *From Carthew Summit, the magnificent view into Glacier National Park, Montana.*

BOTTOM: *The route to the high point south of Carthew Summit. Photo Daniel Yang*

Going farther to Mount Carthew (very steep hiking and some easy scrambling)

A totally outstanding viewpoint. Numerous peaks of Waterton and Glacier national parks are clearly visible.

DISTANCE ADD 3.4 KM RETURN FROM THE COL

HEIGHT GAIN ADD 320 M

HIGH POINT 2630 M

VERY STRENUOUS LENGTH AND STEEPNESS

1. From Carthew Summit ascend the ridge going northwest to the false summit of Mount Carthew. It's a steep grind most of the way up.

2. Continue following the ridge, now in a northeast direction, to the true summit of Carthew and a magnificent view. Some minor scrambling required. Return the same way you came in.

Going farther to Mount Alderson (very steep hiking, some easy scrambling, and route-finding)

Unquestionably one of the premier hikes/ scrambles in the park. Stunning rock, scenery and views throughout!

DISTANCE ADD 5.2 KM RETURN FROM THE COL

HEIGHT GAIN ADD 460 M

HIGH POINT 2692 M

VERY STRENUOUS LENGTH AND STEEPNESS

1. Like Mount Carthew, the route up Alderson is obvious, even though there is little to no trail. From Carthew Summit descend the trail going east towards the west ridge of Alderson.

2. Near the low point, leave the trail and start up the west ridge. There are two obstacles on the ridge to get around. First you will eventually arrive at a severe drop-off. Back up and find an easy path on the left (north) side of the ridge. The second obstacle (the crux) occurs later when a drop-off forces you to find a way down a rock band, this time on the right side. Look for cairns and be sure to find a route that is no more than easy scrambling. Beyond this point, the ascent is easy and straightforward. Expect to take at least 2 hours from the col to the summit.

3. As well as taking in the unbeatable summit view, it is worth it to descend the southeast ridge for a short distance until an excellent view of Bertha Lake is revealed. Return the same way you came in.

TOP: *The summit view towards Mount Alderson. Alderson Lake is nestled below its namesake mountain. Photo Steve Patitsas*

BOTTOM: *The sensational view of Mount Alderson from the col. Photo Mark Nugara*

OPPOSITE: *From Carthew Summit, the route to Mount Carthew goes up the ridge on the left and then traverses to the true summit at the right. Photo Daniel Yang*

93

TOP: *Looking back at the colourful first drop-off. Thankfully, you don't have to down-climb this!*
BOTTOM: *The view from the top.*

20 Carthew–Alderson Lakes

Just over 13 km of some of the most scenic hiking you may ever do! Wait for a perfect weather day.

Note: *It is necessary to take the shuttle or get a ride to Cameron Lake. This hike starts at Cameron Lake but ends in the townsite, at Cameron Falls. For shuttle information call Tamarack Outdoor Outfitters at 403-859-2378 or email info@tamarackwaterton.com.*

DISTANCE 20.1 KM ONE WAY

HEIGHT GAIN 650 M

HIGH POINT 2311 M

STRENUOUS

SUMMER

START: Drive 16 km to Cameron Lake, at the end of Akamina Parkway.

DIFFICULTY: Great signed trail all the way. Some sections of scree and steep terrain.

---

1. Follow the directions to Carthew Summit (page 90). This will be the highest point of the trip.

2. After taking in the spectacular view of the Carthew Lakes, sandwiched between mounts Carthew and Alderson, continue on the trail, down the east side of the col.

3. Follow the trail past the Carthew Lakes and then down to Alderson Lake. This section is arguably the highlight of the hike.

4. Unfortunately the final 7 km of the hike, from Alderson Lake to the townsite, is somewhat anticlimactic, with limited views, but at least it's all downhill and the trip ends at beautiful Cameron Falls.

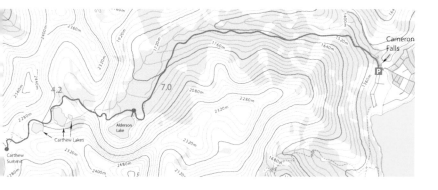

TOP: *One of the best views in Waterton Park: Mount Alderson and the three Carthew Lakes. Note the trail down to the lakes. Photo Steve Patitsas*

BOTTOM: *Approaching the first of the beautiful Carthew Lakes. The trail goes around the left side of the lake. Photo Robert and Robin Charlton*

TOP: *Almost at the second lake.*

BOTTOM: *Alderson Lake appears.*

WATERTON TOWNSITE

Most of the hikes that start from the townsite feature fantastic and immediate views of the three Waterton lakes. Crypt Lake is a classic trip that should be on every hiker's to-do list. The much shorter Bear's Hump features a breathtaking view of the townsite, lakes and surrounding mountains.

Enjoying the stellar view of the Waterton townsite as seen from the summit of the Bear's Hump. Photo Mark Nugara

21 Bear's Hump

The most popular hike in the park. A good short workout to an amazing viewpoint above the townsite.

DISTANCE 2.4 KM RETURN

HEIGHT GAIN 225 M

HIGH POINT 1525 M

MODERATE

LATE SPRING, SUMMER, EARLY FALL

START: From the park gate, drive 7.3 km and turn right, into the unsigned parking lot.

DIFFICULTY: Excellent trail throughout. Steep in places, but rock steps make travel a little easier. Expect lots of people on the trail.

1. The trailhead is clearly marked and there is only one way to go. A relatively gentle grade soon gives way to steeper terrain. It's 1.2 km from bottom to top.

2. The expansive summit offers excellent views in all directions. Be careful about getting too close to the edge and DO NOT throw rocks down. Rock climbers routinely make their way up the face below the summit. Return the same way you came in.

3. Optional: to get some extra exercise and a higher viewpoint, it is possible to hike/scramble a short distance up the south ridge of Mount Crandell on very solid rock that is fun to climb. The route is obvious, but only go as far as the first, significantly steep rock band. The terrain above involves difficult, exposed scrambling and route-finding challenges.

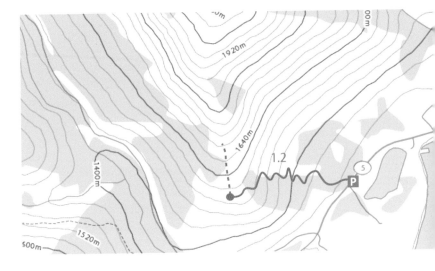

Kian and Rogan Nugara hike the lower section of the new Bear's Hump trail. Photo Mark Nugara

Kian and Rogan also enjoying the awesome rock of the extension up the south ridge of Mount Crandell. Photo Mark Nugara

22 Linnet Lake and trails

The easiest trail in the park. Options to hike alongside the Middle/Upper lakes and go to the famous Prince of Wales Hotel.

DISTANCE 1 KM LOOP

HEIGHT GAIN MINIMAL

EASY

YEAR-ROUND IF NOT ICY

START: From the park gate, drive 6.8 km and turn left into the Linnet Lake parking lot.

DIFFICULTY: A wheelchair-accessible, paved trail around the lake. Several easy and good trails to the Prince of Wales Hotel. No trail following the shore of Middle Waterton Lake.

1. Follow the paved trail around the lake in either direction. There are good views of Mount Crandell from the east side of the lake and of Vimy Peak and the Prince of Wales Hotel from the west side. The information signs along the way are very interesting.

Going farther to the Prince of Wales Hotel

A scenic stroll to one of the most famous hotels in the province.

DISTANCE ADD 2 KM

HEIGHT GAIN ADD 50 M

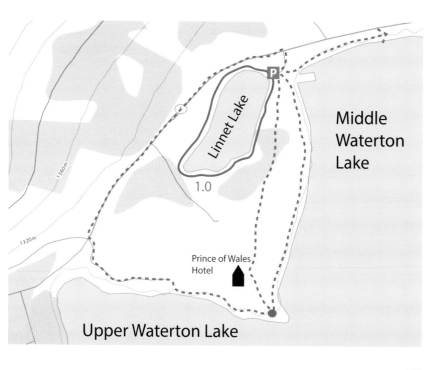

TOP: *Skye Nugara looks pretty happy to be at the lake. Her brother Rogan is already checking things out. Photo Keri Nugara*

BOTTOM: *Somewhat sheltered from the wind, Linnet Lake is more likely to offer good lake reflections, like this one of Vimy Peak.*

TOP: *The trail just above Upper Waterton Lake.*

BOTTOM: *The iconic Prince of Wales Hotel from the upper trail.*

1. After circling the lake, find the hiking trail sign at the northeast end of the lake and follow the trail as it goes south, just above Upper Waterton Lake, to a point below the Prince of Wales Hotel.

2. Either take the trail up to the hotel and then follow the upper trail back to the Linnet Lake or continue around the lakeshore to the picnic areas southwest of the hotel (recommended for the rock scenery). Return the same way you came in or hike alongside the road back to the Linnet Lake parking lot.

Going farther along the Middle Lake shore

Easy lakeshore hiking to extend your day and enjoy the lake.

TOP: *This little peninsula of rock is another one of my favourite spots in the park.*

BOTTOM: *Looking along the route.*

OPPOSITE: *The sun-bleached driftwood on the lakeshore is part of the ecosystem and should not be removed.*

DISTANCE VARIABLE

HEIGHT GAIN NONE

1. Following the shore of Middle Lake eastward is a terrific way to spend an hour or two, especially on a sunny morning. Views of the lake, surrounding mountains and the Prince of Wales Hotel are terrific. There is no trail – simply follow the lakeshore as far as you like and then return the same way you came.

23 Crypt Lake

Take a boat ride across the lake, hike past several waterfalls, crawl through a tunnel, traverse the edge of a precipitous cliff with a chain to grab onto, and arrive at a beautiful lake – a must-do trip for all hikers. This hike has been on National Geographic's list of 20 Best Hikes in the World.

DISTANCE 17.4 KM RETURN

HEIGHT GAIN 675 M

HIGH POINT 1980 M

STRENUOUS

SUMMER

START: Drive into the townsite and turn left at the 3-way stop, onto Mount View Road. Drive to the end and turn left onto Waterton Avenue, where the marina parking lot sits. Arrive early (7:30 am in the summer) to ensure you get a spot on the boat, or buy your tickets the day before.

DIFFICULTY: The most varied hike in the park. Mostly an easy, signed trail, but with more-challenging, rocky terrain with exposure near the lake.

NOTE: Boat departure times vary throughout the season. Call the Waterton Shoreline Cruise Co., 403-859-2362, for schedules and availability.

1. Enjoy the relaxing and scenic 15-minute boat ride across the lake to Crypt Landing. **Note the return times for the boats.** Missing the last departure means you will have to hike 40+ km around all three Waterton lakes to get back to the townsite.

2. The 8.7 km Crypt Lake trail is well signed and easy to follow. Since solitude is unlikely, you will have plenty of fellow hikers to latch onto! This is prime bear habitat, so make lots of noise and hike in a group if possible. While a light-speed hiking pace is unnecessary, you will want to move at a moderate pace to ensure you have plenty of time to stop and take in some of the highlights of the trip, including:

- Twin Falls, Burnt Rock Falls, Crypt Falls
- the tunnel
- the chain section – quite exposed, for those not used to such situations
- the lake
- a potential hike around the lake

3. Upon reaching Crypt Lake, if time permits, there is the option to hike around the lake in either direction. Check the time often! Return the same way you came in.

4. The optional side trip to Hell-Roaring Falls is recommended on return if you have the time.

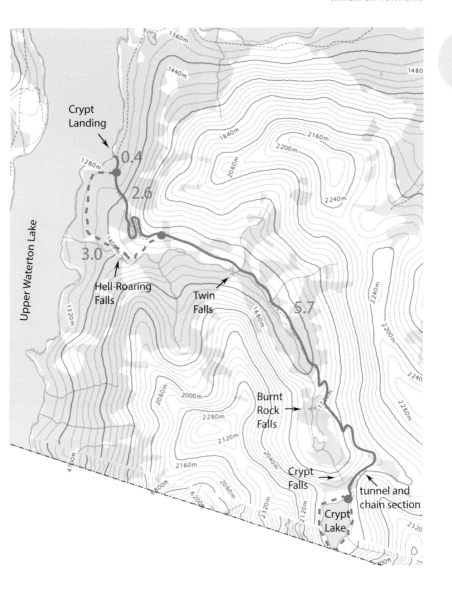

Crypt Landing

0.4

2.6

3.0

Upper Waterton Lake

Hell-Roaring Falls

Twin Falls

5.7

Burnt Rock Falls

Crypt Falls

tunnel and chain section

Crypt Lake

LEFT: *Fun in the tunnel.*

ABOVE: *The chain section. Most will have a pretty tight grip on the chain throughout! Photo Nicole Lisafeld*

BOTTOM: *Crypt Lake from the left (east) side of the lake.*

24 Waterton Lakeshore

More of a walk than a hike, but a great way to see the Upper Lake and the townsite.

DISTANCE VARIABLE

HEIGHT GAIN MINIMAL

VERY EASY

YEAR-ROUND

START: Drive into the townsite and turn left at the 3-way stop, onto Mount View Road. At the end of the road turn left onto Waterton Avenue, where the marina parking lot sits.

DIFFICULTY: Either a paved path near the lakeshore or no trail at all along the gravel beach.

1. Make your way over to the lakeshore and start following it south, either on the paved path or right alongside the water. Go as far as you like. After using a bridge to cross Cameron Creek, you will come to the end of the line. For the very adventurous, when the water is low it is possible to continue a little farther onto the rocky terrain by the lake, for additional views. Use extreme caution.

2. On return, there are multiple options to go through the townsite, where you can grab an ice cream or a delicious gourmet hot dog from Wieners of Waterton!

Pick the paved path or the pebbled lakeshore. Photo Kari Peters

TOP: *Views of Vimy Peak are excellent throughout. (It's unlikely, however, that you'll see my parents, two of my aunts and my uncle!)*

BOTTOM: *A couple of the real denizens of Waterton cross Cameron Creek, near where it empties into Upper Waterton Lake. Photo Marko Stavric*

25 Bertha Lake

An excellent workout to a pristine lake, with a couple of waterfalls en route.

DISTANCE 10.4 KM RETURN

HEIGHT GAIN 460 M

HIGH POINT 1780 M

STRENUOUS

SUMMER, EARLY FALL

START: Drive into the townsite and go straight at the 3-way stop. Follow Evergreen Avenue past Cameron Falls and to the signed Bertha Lake parking lot on the right.

DIFFICULTY: Good, signed trail all the way to the lake. A few steeper sections and lots of switchbacks higher up.

1. Hike 1.5 km to a junction just before the first trail sign. Go left for a very short distance to Bertha Lookout and a terrific view of Upper Waterton Lake and Mount Cleveland.

2. Return to the junction and continue on the trail for a few metres to the next trail sign.

3. Take the fork for Bertha Lake (3.7 km away). Stop along the way to check out Lower Bertha Falls (take the left fork 1.1 km from the turnoff) and Upper Bertha Falls (about 3 km from the turnoff). The Upper Falls are quite distant and not easy to see through the trees. After enjoying some lakeshore views, either hike around the lake or return the same way you came in.

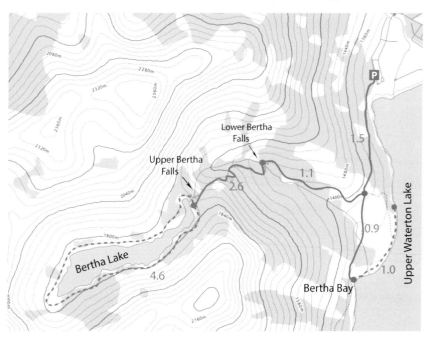

Going farther, around the lake

If you are at the lake, might as well go around it!

DISTANCE ADD 4.6 KM

HEIGHT GAIN 50 M

1. Follow the trail around the lake in either direction, though going clockwise eliminates any confusion when passing by the Bertha Lake campground. The summits surrounding the lake, in a clockwise direction, are Mount Richards, Mount Alderson and Bertha Peak.

ABOVE: *Enjoying the view of Upper Waterton Lake and Mount Cleveland, before the Kenow fire. It's even better now after the fire! Photo Marko Stavric*

LEFT: *Lower Bertha Falls.*

OPPOSITE: *The summertime shore of Bertha Lake.*

TOP: *A winter view of Bertha Lake.*

BOTTOM: *Karen, Jill and Ryan Alston and Reggie Williams hike one of the scenic stretches that goes right along the lakeshore.*

TOP: *The usually skittish wildlife was not so skittish on this day. This little fellow came out of nowhere and strolled right by Reggie.*

BOTTOM: *The lake boasts two red argillite beaches. This one is on the northwest shore. Great place for a dip on a hot summer day.*

26 Bertha Bay

Explore a small section of the shores of Upper Waterton Lake, away from the crowds in the townsite.

DISTANCE 4.6 KM RETURN

HEIGHT GAIN 250 M

MODERATE

SPRING, SUMMER, FALL

START: From the 3-way stop, go straight and follow Evergreen Avenue past Cameron Falls and on to the signed Bertha Lake trailhead.

DIFFICULTY: Good, signed trail all the way.

For map, see page 113, Bertha Lake.

1. Hike 1.5 km to a junction just before the first trail sign. Go left for a very short distance to Bertha Lookout and a terrific view of Upper Waterton Lake and Mount Cleveland.

2. Return to the junction and continue for a few metres to a trail sign.

3. Turn left and follow the 900 m length of the path going down to Bertha Bay and a pleasant spot on the shore of Upper Waterton Lake.

TOP: *An early-winter view across the lake from Bertha Bay. The lake hadn't frozen over yet. In some years it doesn't freeze at all.*

BOTTOM: *The Bertha Creek crossing. Using the log was tenuous at best. I put on hip waders for the return trip!*

OPPOSITE: *A wintery close-up look at Mount Cleveland, in Glacier National Park, and Upper Waterton Lake. Photo Steve Patitsas*

A comparison of the wildly varying water levels of Upper Waterton Lake is seen in these photos taken in January and June 2017. Note that the log at the far left of the winter photo is the same one that is the focus of the late spring photo.

The end of the line. Even with hip waders, travel beyond this point was way too dangerous, especially given the windy and therefore wavy conditions.

Going farther along the lakeshore

DISTANCE ADD 2 KM RETURN

HEIGHT GAIN MINIMAL

1. Provided the lake is relatively low and you can cross nearby Bertha Creek, follow the shoreline north, taking in unique views of Vimy Peak and Mount Boswell. Some short sections of minor scrambling may be required if you want to keep your feet dry. At various times of the year you can go a fair distance, but steep, cliffy terrain eventually stops progress. Return the same way you came in.

27 Alderson Lake

A quicker way to see Alderson Lake than the route from Cameron Lake, though not as scenic unless you continue to Carthew Lakes and Summit, in which case it's spellbinding!

DISTANCE 14 KM RETURN

HEIGHT GAIN 575 M

HIGH POINT 1875 M

MODERATE TO STRENUOUS

LATE SPRING, SUMMER, EARLY FALL

START: Drive into the townsite and at the three-way stop go straight. Follow Evergreen Avenue to the Cameron Falls parking area.

DIFFICULTY: Good, maintained trail all the way.

For map, see page 95, Carthew-Alderson Lakes.

1. The trailhead sits right at the parking area. Follow the trail for 7 km to Alderson Lake and campground. The trail runs high above Carthew Creek for most of the distance and eventually veers south and follows Alderson Creek. Just before the campground, turn left at a signed junction and go 300 m to the campground. The lake is a short walk from there.

Not a bad starting point! Cameron Falls marks the start of the trip to Alderson Lake. Photo Kari Peters

TOP: *The peaceful waters of Alderson Lake early in the morning.*

BOTTOM: *Too early! A late-May trip can still yield amazing winter-like views of the lake and surrounding mountains from above the lake's east side.*

2. Optional: from the lakeshore it is possible to gain a little elevation above the lake's east side. There, you are granted excellent views of Mount Carthew and Buchanan Peak.

3. Return the same way you came in or continue to the Carthew Lakes (highly recommended).

Going farther to Carthew Lakes and Carthew Summit

The path to the stunning Carthew Lakes and the even more stunning viewpoint of Carthew Summit is easy to follow from Alderson Lake. Note, however, that unless you have pre-arranged a car pickup at Cameron Lake, you will have to return the same way. See the Summit Lake and the Carthew–Alderson Lakes trips (pages 88 and 95) for maps.

ABOVE: *Checking out this significant waterfall up close on the right side of the valley is a great little side trip.*

OPPOSITE TOP: *Idyllic is the only word that can describe the environs of the Carthew Lakes.*

OPPOSITE BOTTOM: *The cirque below Carthew Summit that leads to Summit Lake and then down to Cameron Lake. Photo Robert and Robin Charlton*

DISTANCE ADD 3.3 KM TO LOWER
CARTHEW LAKE PLUS 1.9 KM TO
CARTHEW SUMMIT

HEIGHT GAIN ADD 300 M TO LOWER
CARTHEW LAKE PLUS 140 M TO
CARTHEW SUMMIT

HIGH POINT 2311 M

1. The trail continues past Alderson Lake and then up the headwall to Lower Carthew Lake.

2. The extra 1.9 km to Carthew Summit is well worth the effort, as it grants you a spectacular view over the Carthew Lakes, with mounts Carthew and Alderson on either side. Return the same way you came in, unless you have booked a return trip from Cameron Lake back to the townsite. If that is the case, from Carthew Summit, follow the trail west to Summit Lake and then down to Cameron Lake. Also note that ascents of mounts Carthew and/or Alderson are options at this point (see pages 90 and 95 for details).

ADDITIONAL ROUTES

This section covers the remainder of the Waterton hikes. The route to the summit of Vimy Peak is one of the longer trips in the book but grants you a unique and outstanding view of the Waterton area. True masochists will continue to Vimy Ridge! For those who like to cycle, Kootenai Brown Trail is an excellent ride with several great viewpoints along the way.

A sublime view of Crypt Lake and Montana's Mount Cleveland as seen from Vimy Ridge.
Photo Vern Dewit

28 Horseshoe Basin Loop Trail

Trek into a beautiful valley lined with picturesque mountains. Opportunities to reach the tops of two peaks. The full loop is optional.

DISTANCE 21.3 KM LOOP

HEIGHT GAIN 670 M

HIGH POINT 1775 M

STRENUOUS

LATE SPRING, SUMMER, EARLY FALL

START: Drive 2 km north of the turn-off into the park and turn left into the Bison Paddock. Drive 1.5 km to the end of the road (do not enter the paddock itself).

DIFFICULTY: Signed trail throughout. Varying terrain from dirt to rocky scree. A few indistinct sections north of the col if you are completing the loop route.

1. Go through the gate, hike around the sometimes dried-up tarn and then head north a short distance to the Horseshoe Basin Loop trail sign.

2. The loop can be done in either direction, but clockwise is recommended (left at the sign) and described here.

3. In about 400 m turn right, onto the Horseshoe Basin Loop trail. The trail winds its way up to the valley above, then gradually descends to a sometimes dried-up creek.

4. Cross the creek and then follow a few switchbacks up the embankment, eventually turning north.

The gradual descent to the creek. The trail goes way over to the left side and then swings back to the right after crossing the creek. The significant mountain in front is unofficially named "Rogan Peak." Photo Steve Patitsas

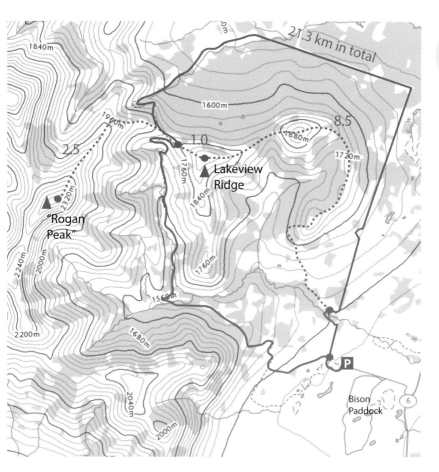

5. Follow the trail up the valley and then up a series of long switchbacks to the col between Lakeview Ridge (east) and unofficial "Rogan Peak" (southwest). This is the high point of the Horseshoe Basin trail, but there are a couple of options to reach better viewpoints, as described later. At this point, you also have the option to return the same way you came instead of completing the full loop route.

6. For the continuation of the Horseshoe Basin trail, continue following the track as it now descends the northwest side of the col, again through a series of switchbacks.

7. Descend all the way down to the open meadows below. A couple of markers and hiking signs help as you go northeast and then east. The trail is indistinct in a few places.

8. The trail eventually joins up with the obvious cutline going due east, then due south. A crossing of Galwey Brook is required near the south end.

9. Finish the day with a drive (no hiking here!) around the Bison Paddock.

Going farther to Lakeview Ridge (some minor scrambling required)

Straightforward ascent to a fine viewpoint – a must-do route if you've made it this far. Expect some minor scrambling.

TOP: *On the switchbacks to the col, much of the route to "Rogan Peak" (just right of centre) is visible. Photo Vern Dewit*

BOTTOM: *Bison, as seen from the safety of your car!*

TOP: *Looking up the west ridge of Lakeview Ridge, on the right. The peak at the left is part of the Lakeview Ridge Horseshoe Loop route. Photo Vern Dewit*

BOTTOM: *Winter ascents of Lakeview Ridge can be extremely rewarding. They provide very distinctive scenery and an experience completely different from summer ascents. From the summit of Lakeview Ridge, the route up "Rogan Peak" (far left) is clearly visible.*

DISTANCE ADD 2 KM RETURN FROM THE LAKEVIEW/"ROGAN" COL

HEIGHT GAIN ADD 150 M

HIGH POINT 1945 M

VERY STRENUOUS STEEPNESS AND LENGTH

1. The route is obvious. Hike east, up the ridge to the summit. There are a few sections where you will have to leave the ridge and circumvent steeper terrain by going to the right.

2. Enjoy the view and then return the same way you came in or complete the loop route.

TOP: *Heading east towards the next major high point (far left) along the horseshoe. Photo Dave McMurray*

BOTTOM: *Bob Spirko checks out an interesting rock formation along the ridge. Photo Dinah Kruze*

TOP: *Descending from the last high point. Go down into the valley and then take a sharp left to the east. Photo Dave McMurray*

BOTTOM: *The deceivingly long ridge of "Rogan Peak." Photo Vern Dewit*

TOP: *The snow viciously blowing off the mountain indicates how strong the winds in Waterton can get. Photo Brad Orr*

BOTTOM: *A great panoramic view just before the summit. Photo Vern Dewit*

Completing the Lakeview Ridge Horseshoe route

Another "full-meal-deal" route that gives you "best bang for your buck." Long, but fantastic ridgewalk. Minor scrambling and route-finding required.

> **DISTANCE ADD 8.5 KM TO THE PARK-ING LOT**
>
> **HEIGHT GAIN ADD 300 M**
>
> **VERY STRENUOUS STEEPNESS AND LENGTH**

1. From the summit of Lakeview Ridge follow the obvious ridge going east down to a low col. Hike up steep terrain to the next high point (about 1920 m).

2. The ridge then curves around to the south. Again the direction is obvious and travel is easy.

3. Go all the way to the last high point of the loop at the far south end. Along the way enjoy some spectacular rock scenery on the left (east) side of the peak.

4. From the last high point, continue following the ridge, now going in a southwest direction, taking the path of least resistance down to the valley below. Here is where the route-finding occurs. The goal is to lose elevation and then swing around to the southeast and find a good trail that parallels Galwey Brook but high above it. The trail eventually descends to the brook, where it intersects the Horseshoe Basin Loop trail. Cross the brook (water levels vary throughout the year and may require a ford) and follow the Horseshoe Basin Loop trail as it ascends the embankment on the other side of the stream and then goes easily back to the start.

Going farther to "Rogan Peak"

The most strenuous of the extensions of this trip, but well worth the effort.

> **DISTANCE ADD 5 KM RETURN FROM THE LAKEVIEW/"ROGAN" COL**
>
> **HEIGHT GAIN ADD 655 M**
>
> **HIGH POINT 2442 M**
>
> **VERY STRENUOUS STEEPNESS AND LENGTH**

1. The route is generally obvious, but not as straightforward as Lakeview Ridge and with significantly more elevation gain. From the Lakeview/"Rogan" col, hike and scramble west, southwest and then south-southwest to the summit. Expect snippets of trail, but lots of steep, trail-less travel and route-finding, mostly on the right side, to get around a few obstacles. Also, expect to take 1.5–2.5 hours to get to the top.

2. Enjoy the outstanding views of many of the most prominent peaks not only in Waterton but also in Glacier National Park, Montana, and then return the same way you came in.

29 Bellevue Hill

Mostly a very steep, off-trail hike/scramble to a relatively low summit with surprisingly impressive views.

DISTANCE 12 KM RETURN

HEIGHT GAIN 900 M

HIGH POINT 2116 M

VERY STRENUOUS STEEPNESS

LATE SPRING, SUMMER, EARLY FALL

START: Drive 2 km north of the turnoff into the park and turn left into the Bison Paddock. Drive 1.5 km to the end of the road (do not enter the paddock itself). Note: if you plan on traversing the mountain over to Red Rock Parkway, leaving a second vehicle at the Bellevue trailhead will save you about 4.5 km of easy hiking at the end of the day.

DIFFICULTY: Signed trail for the first section, then very steep off-trail hiking to the summit. Some route-finding required and varied rocky terrain throughout.

1. Go through the gate and hike around the sometimes dried-up tarn.

2. Hike north a short distance to the HORSESHOE BASIN LOOP TRAIL sign and turn left.

3. In about 400 m turn right, onto the Horseshoe Basin Loop trail. The trail winds its way up to the valley above and the base of the northeast ridge of Bellevue Hill.

4. When you reach the high point, leave the trail by turning left (southwest), and hike up the northeast ridge, through light forest. There is no trail from here to the summit, but the route is obvious. The terrain gets steep quickly. Persevere up this foreshortened slope – it is the steepest part of the trip. A few rock bands are encountered along the way but are easily circumvented on the right side. Note that as of 2021 this

Mark, Rogan and Kian Nugara hike around the tarn at the beginning of the trip. The northeast ridge of Bellevue Hill goes from right to left. A full traverse ends at the left side, near Red Rock Parkway.

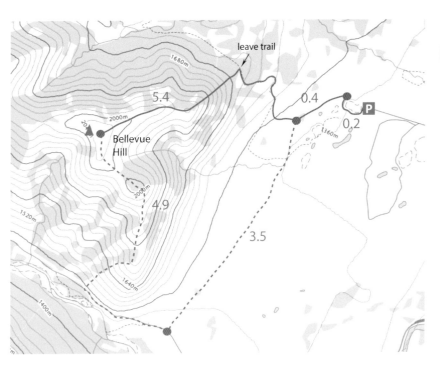

Ascending typically steep terrain on the northeast ridge. Results of the 2017 Kenow fire are still evident for now. Photo Mark Nugara

slope was littered with burned-out trees. As the forest regrows, it may become more challenging to ascend.

5. From the false summit (big cairn) continue travelling west, over the undulating ridge. The true summit sits about 1.4 km southwest of the false summit. Return the same way you came in or continue towards Red Rock Parkway (for experienced hikers/scramblers comfortable with route-finding).

Going farther to complete the loop route via the south ridge

A superb extension for the adventurous and advanced hiker/scrambler that combines Bellevue Hill and the Bellevue Prairie trail.

DISTANCE ADD 9 KM FROM SUMMIT TO PARKING LOT.

STRENUOUS LENGTH AND STEEPNESS

1. From the summit, hike down the obvious south ridge for about 400 m and then turn east to make your way down to a minor high point with a big cairn.

2. Resume travel in a south direction and follow the ridge all the way down to Red Rock Parkway, trending right as you near the road. Expect a few sections of very steep terrain and some route-finding. For those comfortable with route-finding on very steep terrain, the east face of Bellevue is a geologist's dream of exposed, colourful rock. You can swing out onto the east face a few hundred vertical metres before reaching the road and then descend to the Bellevue Prairie trail.

3. Hike back along the road to the Bellevue trailhead and then, on that trail, along the base of Bellevue Hill, back to the start (see Bellevue Prairie Trail North on page 141 for a full description). Alternatively, hike along the road to the Bellevue trailhead and hop into the vehicle you have conveniently left there.

4. Finish the day with a drive (no hiking here!) around the Bison Paddock.

TOP: *Mark Nugara hikes down towards the minor high point on the south ridge at the far left.*

BOTTOM: *Typical terrain down the south ridge. Ruby Ridge is at the far left (see page 60).*

OPPOSITE: *Four happy hikers at the summit: Nugara, Ford, Kazmierczak and Bou. Self-timed photo Sonny Bou*

TOP: *Some of the outrageous rock layers on the east side of Bellevue's south ridge.*

BOTTOM: *The scenic rewards of the detour around the east face of Bellevue Hill. Photo Mark Nugara*

30 Bellevue Prairie Trail North

A good route to access the east end of Red Rock Parkway when the Parkway is closed. Sunrise trips can be very illuminating!

Near the beginning of the trip, the tarn can be full or completely dry. The route goes from right to left, under the fascinating east side of the Hill.

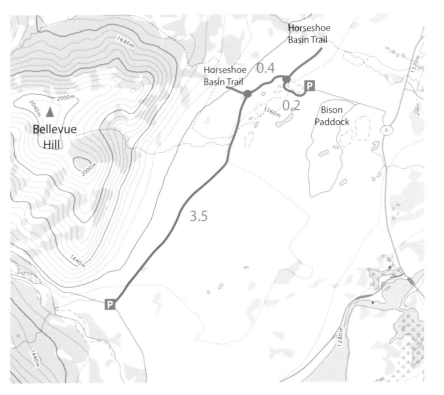

The exposed layers of rock on the east face of Bellevue Hill are some of the most striking and colourful in the park.

DISTANCE 8.2 KM RETURN

HEIGHT GAIN MINIMAL

HIGH POINT 1350 M

EASY

YEAR ROUND

START: Drive 2 km north of the turnoff into the park and turn left into the Bison Paddock. Drive 1.5 km to the end of the road (do not enter the paddock itself).

DIFFICULTY: Easy, signed trail. Indistinct for one short section, but it's easy to get back on the trail.

1. Go through the gate and hike around the sometimes dried-up tarn.

2. Hike north a short distance to the HORSE-SHOE BASIN LOOP TRAIL sign and turn left.

3. The next trail sign, which is also the last, is a short distance along and directs you to go south along the obvious trail (RED ROCK PARKWAY). The trail is sometimes faint, but always obvious.

4. Follow the trail 3.5 km south to Red Rock Parkway, enjoying great views of Bellevue Hill to the west, the foothills and prairies to the east and Waterton to the south. Return the same way you came in.

31 Kootenai Brown Trail

Hike or (preferably) bike a paved walkway alongside the road, with great views over the Lower and Middle Waterton lakes.

DISTANCE 13.8 KM RETURN

HEIGHT GAIN 50 M

HIGH POINT 1320 M

EASY ON BIKE, MODERATE ON FOOT DUE TO OVERALL LENGTH

LATE SPRING, SUMMER, EARLY FALL

NOTE 1: This is a multi-use trail. Give the right of way to faster travellers such as cyclists, skateboarders etc.

NOTE 2: The prevailing west/southwest wind invariably means that cycling from the northeast to the southwest will be more difficult than the reverse. Therefore, the northeast starting point is recommended, because it will be easier on return.

DIFFICULTY: Paved. Great for bikes.

Northeast starting point: Some 700 m past the park gate, turn left at the KOOTENAI BROWN sign and park at the side of the paved trail.

1. Hike or bike 6.9 km to the Linnet Lake parking lot. There are several points of interest along the way and great views throughout. Return the same way you came in.

Southwest starting point: From the park gate drive 6.8 km and turn left into the Linnet Lake parking lot.

1. Hike or bike 6.9 km to the Kootenai Brown picnic area or keep going to the park entrance. There are several points

This trail is great for a family bike ride.
Photo Mark Nugara

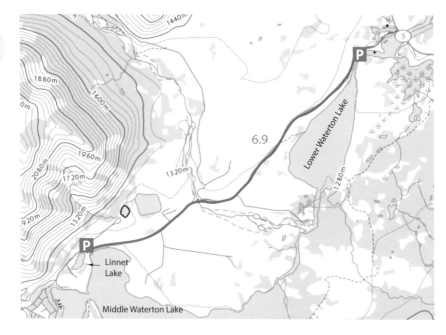

There are plenty of places to see the Prince of Wales Hotel, in front of Mount Richards.

The area just before Linnet Lake makes a great rest and play spot. Photo Mark Nugara

of interest along the way and great views throughout. A picnic area at the Kootenai Brown trailhead provides a good rest spot. Return the same way you came in.

32 Vimy Peak

Another one of the best viewpoints in the park. Not to be missed!

DISTANCE 26.4 KM RETURN

HEIGHT GAIN 1100 M

HIGH POINT 2379 M

VERY STRENUOUS

LATE SPRING, SUMMER, EARLY FALL

START: Drive 0.9 km east of the turnoff into the park and turn right, onto Highway 6. Drive 0.5 km to the trailhead, where there's parking on the left side of the road.

DIFFICULTY: Good, signed trail throughout except for the final 1 km to the top. Steep scree trail to the summit. One creek crossing required.

1. Hike (bike strongly recommended) the relatively flat Wishbone Trail for 7 km. It can be overgrown in places. At the 5.5 km mark, you have to cross Sofa Creek. When the water is high some may choose to leave their bike here instead of carrying or pushing it through the stream.

2. At the 7 km mark a trail sign directs you to turn left onto the Vimy Peak trail. Leave your bike here if you haven't already ditched it. Don't be fooled by the "4.8 km" sign. It's almost 7 km to the summit of Vimy with over 1000 m of elevation gain. Expect to take 2.5–3.5 hours to reach the summit from this point.

Fording Sofa Creek when the water is relatively low. Vimy Peak is dead ahead. Photo Bob Spirko

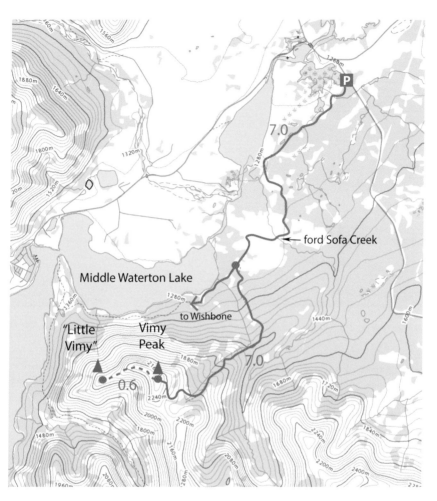

3. Follow the Vimy Peak trail up through thick forest for about 6 km. Two creek crossings are required but are usually very easy on stepping stones.

4. Above treeline the summit of Vimy appears to the west. Stay on the main trail, which veers over to the left and then switchbacks to the right towards the summit. A steeper but more direct trail forks off to the right if that is more to your liking. This trail is great for a faster descent. Expect loose, steep terrain for the upper section, some minor scrambling, and a magnificent summit view. Return the same way you came in or continue to "Little Vimy" and/or Vimy Ridge.

Going farther to "Little Vimy"

Not really a separate peak, just the lower west end of Vimy Peak, offering a much better viewpoint of the Waterton Lakes. Highly recommended.

DISTANCE ADD 1.2 KM RETURN

HEIGHT GAIN ADD 70 M ON RETURN

HIGH POINT 2310 M

147

The final stretch of steep hiking to the summit. Photo Vern Dewit

1. From the summit of Vimy, simply follow the ridge west, down and across to the end of the ridge, about 600 m away. A nearby and slightly lower point offers the best view of the lakes. Return the same way you came in. Continuing along the ridge gets tricky and is not recommended.

Going farther along Vimy Ridge (some scrambling required)

The ultimate extension of the peak. Fantastic views throughout, with options to stop at any of several high points along the way. Expect some scrambling and route-finding.

DISTANCE ADD 10 KM TO THE TRUE SUMMIT AND BACK

HEIGHT GAIN ADD 900 M TO THE TRUE SUMMIT AND BACK

HIGH POINT 2500 M

1. From the summit, follow the ridge south and southeast for as long as you would like. There are three high points to enjoy along the way. The farthest is the true summit of Vimy Ridge, approximately 5 km from Vimy Peak. Otherwise, stop at either of the earlier high points. The unofficially named "Arras Peak" makes for a great objective (see map and photo). Return the same way you came in. Do not attempt any shortcut routes until you are almost back to Vimy Peak (see map and photo).

TOP: *A fantastic summit view, with "Little Vimy" at the left.*

MIDDLE: *Great views over Waterton and beautiful rock all around, throughout the short traverse to "Little Vimy."*

BOTTOM: *Another spellbinding view!*

Starting the long traverse to the summit of Vimy Ridge.
VR *summit of Vimy Ridge.* **A** *Arras Peak.* **MC** *Mount Cleveland (the highest peak in Glacier National Park, Montana). Photo Mark Nugara*

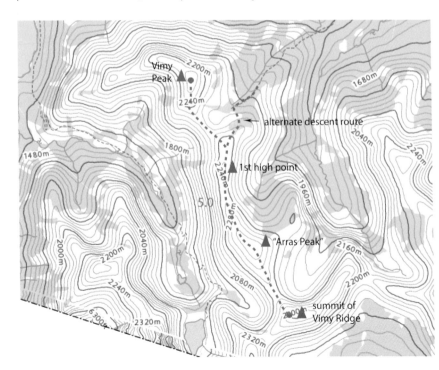

TOP: *The final stretch of terrain to the summit of Vimy Ridge (centre). Photo Vern Dewit*

BOTTOM: *You can take a shortcut at this point by going down to the right. The Vimy Peak trail is in the trees down below. Photo Vern Dewit*

33 Wishbone

A long but scenic trail to a fantastic and unique viewpoint of Waterton. Options to make the trip short or quite long. Biking the first 5.5 km or 7 km of the trail is recommended.

DISTANCE 14.0–28.4 KM RETURN

HEIGHT GAIN 50–300 M

MODERATE TO STRENUOUS

LATE SPRING, SUMMER, EARLY FALL

START: Drive 0.9 km east of the turnoff into the park and turn right, onto Highway 6. Drive 0.5 km to the trailhead.

DIFFICULTY: Good, signed trail throughout. Some rocky terrain on the way to Crypt Landing. One creek crossing required. Some minor scrambling to reach the optional but highly recommended high point.

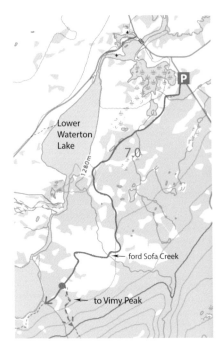

1. Hike (bike recommended) the relatively flat Wishbone Trail for 7 km. It can be overgrown in places. At the 5.5 km mark, you have to cross Sofa Creek. When the water is high some may choose to leave their bike here instead of carrying or pushing it through the stream.

2. At the 7 km mark, a trail sign directs you to take the right fork, continuing along Wishbone Trail. Leave your bike here if you haven't already ditched it.

3. Follow this trail for 4 km to another trail sign for Crypt Landing ("3.2 km"). If you want to see Wishbone Landing, turn right at this sign and follow a slightly fainter trail for a few minutes, down to the lakeshore. Check out the pleasant view of Middle Waterton Lake and then return to the Crypt Landing trail sign.

4. The next 1.4 km of trail is a little harder to follow in places and care should be taken not to lose it. **Note:** my GPS recorded this section as 0.8 km in length, not 1.4 km.

5. At the next trail sign (1.8 km to Crypt Landing), there is the option to hike/scramble up the rocks to the north. This will undoubtedly be the highlight of the entire trip and is not to be missed. The rock here is colourful and remarkably solid (the same rock that the climbing routes on Bear's Hump are comprised of). There is much terrain to explore, and the views over the

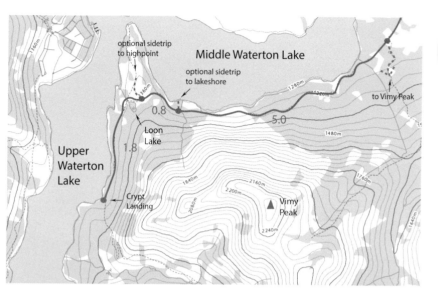

Middle Waterton Lake

optional sidetrip to highpoint

optional sidetrip to lakeshore

to Vimy Peak

Upper Waterton Lake

Loon Lake

Crypt Landing

Vimy Peak

1280m · 1480m · 1760m · 1840m · 2160m · 2200m · 2080m · 2240m · 1140m · 1160m

0.8 · 1.8 · 5.0

Look for some cool rock scenery right before and just after crossing Sofa Creek.

lake to the Waterton townsite and the surrounding mountains are phenomenal. Go back to the trail sign and from there either return the way you came in or continue to Crypt Landing first and then retrace your route in.

Going farther to Crypt Landing

There are several scenic spots to check out as you make your way to the final destination of the day. However, they may seem somewhat anticlimactic if you have seen the view from the rocks as described above.

DISTANCE ADD 3.6 KM RETURN

HEIGHT GAIN ADD 50 M

HIGH POINT 2500 M

1. Follow the trail for 1.8 km to Crypt Landing (my GPS recorded it as 2.3 km). Highlights include: **A**. the shallow but pleasant tarn known as Loon Lake; **B**. a striking band of orange rock to your left just after Loon Lake; **C**. a small bay about halfway there; **D**. the view across the lake from Crypt Landing. Return the same way you came in.

TOP: *Alongside the orange rock (**B**).*

BOTTOM: *The view from Crypt Landing (**D**).*

OPPOSITE TOP: *From atop the rocks there is a unique view of Waterton that few people see.*

OPPOSITE BOTTOM: *A small taste of the colourful rock and stunning views.*

34 Sofa Mountain trail

A very pleasant hike to a partially visible waterfall at the base of Sofa Mountain.

DISTANCE 7.4 RETURN

HEIGHT GAIN 250 M

HIGH POINT 1775 M

EASY

LATE SPRING, SUMMER, EARLY FALL

START: Drive 0.9 km east of the turnoff into the park and turn right, onto Highway 6. Drive 7.2 km and park at the pullout on the right side of the road. The unsigned trail starts here.

DIFFICULTY: Good trail throughout, but sometimes overgrown in places.

1. Hike the well-defined and easy-to-follow trail for about 3.7 km towards Sofa Mountain. There are a few sections where the vegetation on both sides gets quite high (try not to lose the little ones!).

2. The goal is to reach a partially visible waterfall near the base of the mountain. Early in the season, the volume of water pouring down the fall is impressive, but it dries up significantly by midsummer. DO NOT try to scramble down to the base of the waterfall – it's steep, slippery and very dangerous. Return the same way you came in or continue up the valley.

Skye Nugara leads her big brother Kian through open meadows.

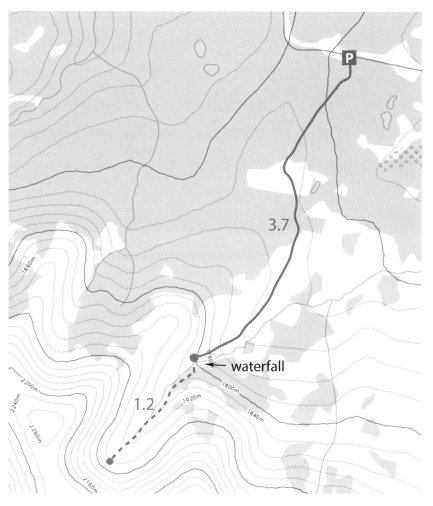

waterfall

Going farther up the valley

Get some extra exercise and see the impressive rock of Sofa Mountain.

DISTANCE ADD 2.4 KM RETURN

HEIGHT GAIN ADD 155 M

HIGH POINT 1930 M

1. The trail does continue up to the valley above the waterfall. Crossing the creek can be difficult when the water is high, but there is a more primitive trail that stays on the right side of the creek.

2. Regardless of which side of the creek you choose, simply follow it up into the bowl below the colourful walls of Sofa Mountain. Go as far as desired and then return the same way you came in. Don't get any overly ambitious ideas about ascending Sofa Mountain from here unless you are an experienced scrambler.

TOP: *The bulk of Sofa Mountain is revealed about halfway along the trail.*

BOTTOM: *Looking down toward the waterfall. Photo Mark Nugara*

TOP: *Lingering snow can make travel easier, but it also adds an element of danger. Use caution if walking on the snow. Photo Mark Nugara*

MIDDLE: *Looking up the valley.*

BOTTOM: *The rock at the far end of the valley is very colourful and strikingly folded in places. Totally worth checking out!*

Contact Information

- Waterton National Park Visitor Centre
  403-859-5133; waterton.info@pc.gc.ca
- Waterton Shoreline Cruise
  Company 403-859-2362;
  cruise.info@watertoncruise.com
- Tamarack Outdoor Outfitters
  403-859-2378;
  info@tamarackwaterton.com

Emergency phone numbers

- Waterton Park Wardens/Fire/Ambulance
  403-859-2636
- RCMP 403-859-2244
- Hospitals: Cardston 403-653-4411, Pincher
  Creek 403-627-3333
- EMERGENCY **911**

Campgrounds

- Waterton Townsite 403-859-5133
- Crandell Mountain 403-859-5133
- Crooked Creek 403-653-1100
- Belly River 403-859-2224

Acknowledgements

Thank you to the following for their photo contributions: Jill Alston, Sonny Bou, Robert and Robin Charlton, Matthew Clay, Vern Dewit, Matthew Hobbs, Naheer Hirji, Stephen Hui, Rafal Kazmierczak, Dinah Kruze, Nicole Lisafeld, Dave McMurray, Keri Nugara, Mark Nugara, Brad Orr, Steve Patitsas, Kari Peters, Bob Spirko, Marko Stavric, Reggie Williams and Daniel Yang. Special thanks once again to Shawn Benbow for his photo-editing expertise.